Brian Edwards
Raising a Teenage Girl
AS A SINGLE DAD
THE ROLLER COASTER RIDE WITH MY SELF-OBSESSED, MOODY AND DEFIANT DAUGHTER

outskirts press

Raising a Teenage Daughter as a Single Dad
The Roller Coaster Ride With My Self-Obssessed,
Moody and Defiant Daughter
All Rights Reserved.
Copyright © 2020 Brian Edwards
v2.0

The opinions expressed in this manuscript are solely the opinions of the author and do not represent the opinions or thoughts of the publisher. The author has represented and warranted full ownership and/or legal right to publish all the materials in this book.

This book may not be reproduced, transmitted, or stored in whole or in part by any means, including graphic, electronic, or mechanical without the express written consent of the publisher except in the case of brief quotations embodied in critical articles and reviews.

Outskirts Press, Inc.
http://www.outskirtspress.com

ISBN: 978-1-9772-1718-9

Cover Photo © 2020 Brian Edwards. All rights reserved - used with permission.

Outskirts Press and the "OP" logo are trademarks belonging to Outskirts Press, Inc.

PRINTED IN THE UNITED STATES OF AMERICA

Table of Contents

Acknowledgements i

Introduction... 1

Objectives 4

Meet Your Teenage Daughter 15

How to Discipline Her 21

How to Make Her More Respectful 31

How Not to Alienate Her and to
Make Her Listen to You............................... 39

How to Get Her to Open Up and
Talk to You.. 45

How to Get the Behavior You Want
Even When You Are Not There 61

How to Help Her Choose Better Friends.... 69

How to Help Her Make Better Decisions with Boyfriends 77

How to Make Her Want to Progress and Try in School 86

How to Get Her to Do Her Chores 99

How Not to Let Her Be Affected by Peer Pressure 109

How to Get Her to Be More Responsible ... 122

How to Deal with Sex and Drugs 133

How to Introduce Her to Your New Relationships 142

How to Deal with the Roller Coaster of Emotional Issues 151

What to Do When Nothing Works 163

Acknowledgements

I HAVE TO start by thanking my amazing friend Junior who believed in me and gave me the kick I needed to pull the trigger and get this book published. Your friendship throughout the years mean more than you know.

Next I would like to thank Kat for reading the carelessly disorganized unfinished draft and seeing a nugget of something that could be useful to someone else going through the same circumstance. Your unwavering support, encouragement and candid feedback were instrumental in getting me to this point. Without you this book probably would not have happened.

Next, I would like to thank Goran for selflessly giving of his time and patience in getting just the right shots for the covers.

Next, I would like to thank Carolyn for reading the initial draft and suggesting additional topics. Your spirituality and introspection give you a unique perspective of the world and it comes out in everything you do.

Finally, I would like to thank my beautiful daughter. Watching you grow up has been the singular greatest pleasure in my life. To you I say, let passion be your guide in the choices you make but temper it with common sense. You are brilliant, passionate, driven, loyal and independent. You have all of the tools to make your life amazing.

Introduction

ARE YOU A single dad trying your best to raise a teenage daughter? Is she different from the way she was just a few short years ago? Is she becoming closer to her peers and no longer wanting any public displays of affection with you? If so, welcome to the club, my friend.

For me, the change felt like it happened overnight, almost like someone flipped a switch. I awoke one day and there was this stranger living in my house. There was this tectonic personality shift. She would no longer rush home to tell me about her day at school, and any questions about it were met with "fine." Yep, those days of daddy's little angel were over.

Teenagers are unique creatures, not quite child yet not quite adult. Parenting someone at that phase in their lives can be extremely challenging. Sometimes they become secretive, disrespectful, and distant. They go from loving to play dress up and watching *SpongeBob* reruns to suddenly becoming hell-bent on making the same mistakes we made as teenagers.

For a single dad with a girl, it becomes even more challenging. We are unable to give them examples about the specific changes they are going through from our own experience. Also, as guys, we know exactly what's on teenage boys' minds. Every boy's a predator, and girls their prey, on the grasslands of high school.

Because of that, there is the risk of us being overprotective, which could actually drive them away and counteract everything we are trying to do. As adults, we know exactly where that road is heading and would like, as far as possible, for her to avoid the pitfalls we encountered when we were that age.

We initially believe that because we know how we were at that age, we can do a better job than our parents did. The problem is, we are not sure what approach to take. We oscillate between trying to be the hip parent and being the authoritarian. We really want to help her avoid making "permanent" mistakes. Yes, we all know what those "permanent" mistakes are. Yet the more we try, the more we alienate her.

I have learned, by a process of trial and error, to figure out what works for me. Who am I? Sorry, I am not a PhD in child development psychology with tenure at Harvard. I am just a regular single parent of a now-wonderful teenage young woman. It has not always been that way, and we have been through almost every difficulty imaginable.

Somehow, through it all, we are now closer than we have ever been, and I am excited to see the woman she will become.

In the following chapters, I will outline the difficulties I encountered, which I am sure are universal, and the strategies I used to get to this point where she is now—a well-adjusted, hardworking, honest, confident young adult who I am extremely proud of.

Objectives

WHAT ARE WE trying to accomplish with our girls? Before we embark on the journey of parenthood, I believe we as parents need to take a step back and really examine this question. We will realize that our goals may vary from the short to long term. It may even vary based on how they are behaving at the time.

Earlier in her life, I found myself getting angry and frustrated if she did anything wrong, and I sometimes reacted based on those emotions. My reaction—yelling—fixed the initial issues, but they never stayed fixed. Sooner or later, she would revert to doing whatever she had done wrong in the first place. For example, one of the things she had to do on a daily basis was to make her bed when she got up. She would do it for a while but then stop. Once I discovered this and yelled at her, she would start again. This cycle went on day after day and week after week. I had to keep my boot to her neck.

This applied to most things, and I was beginning to wonder if I was teaching her anything. Note, I said "if I was teaching her anything" rather than "if she was learning anything." I specifically use "teaching" because I believe we need to take responsibility for imparting the lessons we give them. If they are not absorbing the lessons, we need to examine our delivery or any other factors that may stop our message from getting through. To me, using the word "learning" implies that it's her fault.

I decided there had to be a better way to ensure long-term success. First, I had to stop reacting and become more proactive in my parenting if I wanted to make any significant difference in her life. I mean, I'm the adult, right? My prefrontal cortex is fully developed;

I could think strategically and figure this out. I am at the top of the evolutionary chain. How hard could this be?

As a parent, I knew intuitively what kind of person I wanted her to become but had never taken the time to really think about it. I was winging it through parenthood, dealing with situations as they arose, and hoping for the best. Without a set direction, I dealt with her transgressions based on how I felt at that moment without consideration of the long-term results. My self-righteous ranting only resulted in short-term results. Clearly, winging it wasn't cutting it.

One of my favorite books is called "The Prophet" by Kahlil Gibran, a Lebanese author. In it he said, "You are the bows from which your children as living arrows are sent forth". I read that many years ago and it resonated with me. My job is to prepare her for the future and I was clearly failing.

I needed to think about this strategically—focus on the long term and work toward that. An epiphany came to me by really unusual means. One day, I was browsing the Red Cross website after the earthquake in Haiti and came across their mission statement.

According to the definitive source, Google, a mission statement is defined as the following: "A formal summary of the aims and values of a company, organization, or individual."

I saw the word "individual" and thought to myself, that was the ultimate in strategic thinking. It works for the Red Cross, so why not me? I mean, if I came up with a mission statement, it would go a long way toward helping me get past the reactionary thinking.

I decided then and there to come up with my own mission statement for raising her. This was extremely important to me, and I did not take it lightly. This statement had to have three characteristics: high level, all-encompassing, and long term. Every subsequent action I took would then be measured against it.

To get started, I ignored the day-to-day issues and pictured the kind of adult I wanted her to become. I looked at the people I considered role models. I also took a candid look at myself and looked at my good points but paid particular attention to my shortcomings. I wanted her to be better than I was.

The statement I eventually came up with went something like this:

> *I want my daughter to be a confident, honest, and responsible adult, someone who has a strong sense of self, is capable of handling failures without self-doubt, and believes she can accomplish anything.*

Note that my statement had nothing to do with tangible success, such as going to college and being a doctor. I focused on what I considered to be qualities that would make a happy and well-adjusted human being who would fit in well with society.

The next step was to determine how I would accomplish this mission. I thought about my actions in the past, how I dealt with her transgressions. Why did I yell at her for breaking the window or not cleaning her room? I yelled because I was angry. Yelling was me taking out my anger on her and had nothing to do with fixing the problem.

Thinking about this made me realize that yelling was only for my benefit. This had nothing to do with her. It just made me feel better by getting my anger out. It was a selfish emotion. Over the years, I had convinced myself that this was parenting. However, that only made her change her actions to avoid me yelling. It did nothing to teach her why she shouldn't do it in the first place.

When I punished her, the goal was not to take my anger out on her so I could feel better. The goal was to teach her a lesson. In society today, the phrase "to teach someone a lesson" has a negative connotation. It implies punishment or revenge. I decided to repurpose the phrase and take it in its literal sense. I then appointed myself "professor," with lifelong tenure.

I looked at her behaviors and broke them down into habits and traits. Habits are the things she has learned, while traits refer to her personality type and innate qualities. I can have an effect on her habits, but trying to change her traits would be like holding my hand up to an incoming wave. My approach needed to take this into consideration. For example, she is very independent. Therefore, she didn't need to be spoon-fed with every instruction. Using that approach would only have annoyed her.

After thinking on this for a while, I determined that the best approach to put my plan into action would be to break down my approach into tasks and lessons. Tasks were the day-to-day things she needed to do that she hated doing. The purpose of this is to try to instill good habits. Here are some examples:

- Keep her room tidy
- Wake up on time for school
- Complete homework on time and turn it in
- Do the dishes
- Dress appropriately

No amount of lecturing or persuasion would have made her do these things. They were also a lot of the reasons I had yelled in the past. I needed to find a way of getting her to do these things without me yelling all the time.

Tasking is something that anyone can do since it involves an authoritarian approach. You tell them what to do, and they do it. It doesn't require a PhD to implement. As I found out and am sure most of you reading this have found out as well, this only works in the short term, and most times, you have to be physically present to enforce it. As soon as your back is turned, it's all over.

Even as adults, we hate performing tasks. They are the necessary evils that need to be performed. If it's hard for us, imagine how difficult it is for a teenager. Looking at it from that perspective, I decided my best approach would be to create strategies to help her get these hateful tasks done. I will outline these strategies later in the book.

Lessons, on the other hand, required me teaching her and having her truly understand what I was trying to impart. She must not just understand; she must also agree. These are tricky in that there is an element of persuasion. I had to make her see that this was truly best for her and get her buy in. If you can pull this off, you're home free. Once a lesson is learned and internalized, you no longer have to be physically present for this behavior to occur. As long as they can see for themselves that something makes sense, their behavior will begin to change. This is the most powerful tool we have, but it is easier said than done.

Trying to teach a lesson without an active term of reference would not have as great an effect as utilizing actual occurrences to make your point. In short, back up your lesson with examples; if you can tell it in the form of a story, it will be so much better. It has been proven that people pay more attention to stories. For example, getting your teen to sit and then telling them that having sex too early is wrong would probably result in a snicker, if not the infamous eye roll. However, showing them an unemployed, homeless teen mom whose boyfriend has left her in a movie or in the news could be your opening.

With this in mind, you have to be vigilant and constantly be on the lookout for lessons. Life is the biggest university of all, and as the parent of its most recent freshman, you are the first professor to help your daughter navigate her campus. Do not let any opportunity for a lesson pass you by.

We need to keep the overarching mission in mind at all times since this will dictate how we handle the many situations that will most certainly arise. A lot of times, we get caught up in the weeds and make short-term decisions that may counter the long-term goal. For example, if you caught her bullying another child or making fun of them, the initial reaction would be to get angry and punish her. The behavior would stop at that point in time. However, she most likely would not stop for long. She would just be more cautious the next time to avoid getting caught.

The better approach would be to use it as a teaching moment and get her to see the consequences of her actions and help her to understand why that type of behavior is unacceptable. I will give further examples in later chapters.

Understand that there will be many deviations along the way as your daughter embarks upon the first leg of the journey into adulthood. The road is not well paved, and most stumble along the way. As her dad, you need to recognize that stumbles are just that: stumbles. Accept that you will not be able to prevent a lot of these missteps and that the most you can do is point them out, help her when she does stumble, and just keep her walking.

Always remember, she is your gift to the world, your legacy. Make sure the world delights in the present.

Meet Your Teenage Daughter

EVERY RELATIONSHIP, GOOD and bad, begins with an introduction. When we meet anyone of consequence to us for the first time, we tend to size them up on both the conscious and the unconscious levels. We look for clues in their words and body language to give us insight into their personality, the goal being to make the interaction a success.

Once the meeting occurs, if a relationship ensues—friendship or otherwise—we eventually fall into complacency, the assumption being that adults' personality traits tend to remain constant over time. Therefore, theoretically, the approach that worked earlier will continue to work throughout the relationship. For example, my good friend who is a fan of the Buffalo Bills, misguided as it may seem, may always have a softness in her heart (and head) for that team.

That state of complacency may begin as soon as a few months after the initial meeting. We have known our teenagers for at least thirteen years. Imagine how entrenched the state of complacency may be after all that time. While adults' personality traits may tend to be fairly static, the teenager is in a constant state of change. Therefore, what worked three, four, or five years ago sure as hell will not work now.

With that in mind, you need to reintroduce yourself to your daughter almost on a daily basis. You need to "*50 First Dates*" her. Throw everything you thought you knew about her out the window. Look at her as you would when meeting a stranger for the first time. Listen to her words and observe her body language, and interpret them with a fresh perspective.

Teenagers universally tend to have similar personality traits. They consist of the following:

- Self-obsessed
- Shortsighted
- Secretive
- Moody
- Defiant

Let's discuss each one in turn and try to shed some light on what they really mean.

Self-Obsessed

In her early teen years, my daughter would not be caught dead outside without doing the proper fifty-point inspection in the mirror. If she had to take out the trash, she would probably cut it back to a forty-point inspection.

That may taste a little like the vanity sauce. However, if we were to look deeper, we would realize that people who are sensitive about how they appear to others tend to be really insecure about themselves.

Shortsighted

Children are notoriously shortsighted. A little kid in the supermarket might run right into you because they were not looking where they were going. This also applies to teenagers in a broader sense. They tend to undertake courses of action that may have serious long-term consequences with abandon.

This is not necessarily their fault. The prefrontal cortex of their brains, which impacts judgment, is not fully developed until at least age twenty. This has been scientifically proven to impair judgment. If you don't believe me, look it up. My daughter once "borrowed" my truck before she had a driver's license, broke the front rim and damaged the suspension, and parked it in the garage. More on that later in the book.

Secretive

There was a time in their lives when they could not wait to tell us everything. In fact, at that stage in their lives, we sometimes wished they would just shut up. That reverses during their teenage years.

They are not really secretive. They are only secretive to us. They tell their friends everything, from their latest crush to the fact that they used a different brand of toothpaste that morning and it was not as minty as the one they used the day before. If you are not sure of this, ask your teenager, on average, how may text messages they send per day, or posts on Instagram.

Moody

Their mood swings are legendary. One second, they are on top of the world, and in an instant, that changes to the "if you even look at me funny, there will be pain" look.

I have read the scientific reasons relating to hormones, etcetera. While that is also true, for me as a teenager, I had an innocence with which I viewed the world. As such, I loved and hated with the same intensity. Eventually, I learned to temper my emotions.

Teenagers have no idea how to do that yet. It just comes with experience.

Defiant

This is the tricky one. We consider them defiant because they do not want to do exactly what we tell them. This goes back to reintroducing yourself to your teenager. Telling them exactly what to do worked in the past. It may not work now.

As we would with every successful relationship, we need to look at all of these characteristics realistically and accept them as part of the reality of who they are. By now, you should have realized that you cannot really change people. You may show them different perspectives, but you cannot change them.

Like every other human being on this planet, they are not perfect. Heck, we aren't exactly straight arrows either.

We need to accept them as individuals with all of their imperfections and also accept that we cannot make them perfect. The most we can hope for is to make them self-aware and give them the desire to take on that responsibility for themselves.

How to Discipline Her

THIS IS ONE of the more controversial topics about raising a teenager. Seems like everyone you speak to has a different take on the topic. Even cultures differ in their approach. The most I can do is give you my take and what has worked for me.

I operate according to the following principles:

- Separate infractions into principles and deeds.
- Be fair.
- Explain why.
- Show the consequences.

- Be consistent.
- Teach, not exact vengeance.

Separate Infractions into Principles and Deeds

Principles relate to anything that would impact her character. I consider these to be the most egregious of infractions since they tend to have the most impact on the type of adult she would become. Examples of these are lying, stealing, bullying, and cheating. My punishment here would be targeted to the behavior, and the punishments would be more of a teaching type rather than something as simple as grounding her. I will give a detailed example later in the chapter.

Deeds relate to things like not doing her chores or being late. These would be met with a simpler type of punishment.

Be Fair

I believe in letting the punishment fit the crime and never trying to insert a thumb tack with a hammer. In my daughter's mind, if the punishment was not fair, she would resent it and rebel. At that point, the punishment would be useless and not achieve anything.

My daughter had a habit of dirtying glasses and leaving them all over the house. I tried talking to her about it, but to no avail. I would get upset, and if I yelled, the issue would get fixed temporarily. Therefore, I had to resort to other means. If I am punishing her, why do I have to be upset? She is the one who needs to feel the pain.

This is what I came up with. I am an early riser, so I told her that I would wake her every time I saw a dirty glass and have her put it where it should be, and then she could go back to bed. I even made a joke about it, in that when I woke her, I made a big production about how it made my day and she needed to leave the glasses out more often so I could have a reason to smile in the morning. Needless to say, that stopped pretty quickly. I did not have to nag her, she was not overly upset, and the objective was achieved. If you can find minor annoyances for your teen to carry out, your job could be made much easier.

Explain Why

I would always explain why I was taking a certain course of action before I took it. Even when I was angry, I would always take the time to explain. I never realized how powerful that was until she told me once, and I quote: "I would like to be angry with you when you punish me, but you always tell me why."

You may think that they don't listen, but now that my daughter is older, I realize that a lot of the things I said actually sunk in. However, the things I didn't say in anger had the best chance of getting through. Once I started off my conversation with anger, her defenses came up and I might as well have been talking to a brick wall.

You, as her dad, have to carefully observe her. I could tell immediately when my "explanations/lectures" were not getting through. She would get a certain glazed look in her eyes, and I would immediately stop and tell her we would continue later when she was paying attention. This would usually perk her up immediately because she sure as hell did not want to hear me droning on a second time.

Show the Consequences with Examples

Part of explaining why is to show her the consequences. Here I would show her what could have happened by her course of action. For example, if she took something she shouldn't have, I would explain not just about going to jail but about the lasting impact it would have on her life. I would put it into her language, like if her friends found her lying, they may no longer trust her or want anything to do with her and she would no longer be "popular." I would even try to see examples around us, such as if something similar happened to one of her friends, in a movie, or in the news. Teaching examples are everywhere. Develop that discerning eye.

Be Consistent

I cannot stress this enough because this is one of the ways you establish structure and gain respect. If you punished her for something she did yesterday and then she did the same thing today, I don't care how much of a hurry you're in, or how tired you are, or if she was exceptionally good for the first part of the day—you have to punish her again. If you don't, she will find ways to manipulate you, and you risk being unable to enforce that action. If she thinks there is a chance of getting away with it, there is the temptation to try her luck. And as stated before, let the punishment fit the crime.

Teach, Not Exact Vengeance

When we punish our girls, we have to ask ourselves if the punishment will help stop the behavior from happening in the future or if it is just that they deserve to be punished and must feel our wrath. We need to examine whether it is a teaching moment or just us dealing out vengeance. The latter just makes the situation worse.

How to Treat Any Situation

These are the steps I took before I reacted to any situation:

1. I first let my anger subside.

2. I asked myself why I was disciplining her and related it to my overarching mission mentioned in the first chapter.
3. I recognized that this is an individual with her own perspectives and tried to place myself in her shoes.
4. I tried to understand why she did what she did.
5. I then decided what course of action to take.

Once, she "borrowed" my truck before she got her driver's license and went for a brief joyride with her friends in the neighborhood. Unfortunately, she hit the curb, broke the front rim, and damaged the front suspension.

She actually had the sense to call me before I came home from work to let me know. In her mind, it was better to have me find out from her instead of discovering it myself. Also, it would give me some time to cool off before I got home.

I am sure you know what I was feeling in that moment. We've all been there. Fortunately, I had that time to cool off before I got home.

She was right to call me. I was able to apply the five-step process before I got home.

1. I was still angry, but I was at least under control.
2. I was definitely going to punish her because what she did wrong and what I was trying to teach her was the following:
   a. Taking something that does not belong to you is wrong, and if she did something like that as an adult, she could go to jail and also lose the respect of her peers.
   b. If you take a course of action that has risk, be sure you can deal with the consequences.
   c. If you have to take extraordinary measures to impress your friends so they will like you, they are not really your friends. Friends should accept you as you are.
3. She is not a mindless drone who does things exclusively to piss me off. There must have been a reason she did what she did.

4. She did it because she wanted to show off for her friends that she could drive. She wanted their acceptance, which is something we never outgrow.
5. Of course I gave her the sermon when I got home, which took into consideration her reasons. In the past when I would go on about how angry I was, I could always see her eyes glaze over. I needed to put it into her language. Because I wanted her to know the consequences of what she did, I then took her through every step I needed to go through to fix the truck, from sourcing the rim to taking it to the repair shop to showing her how much everything cost. I made her understand completely the consequences of her brief moment of pleasure.

In the end, she felt really bad about the whole thing and apologized. It was not the usual "I am sorry to avoid being punished" but a heartfelt apology.

The human reaction to something like that

would have been to get angry, yell at her about being thoughtless and irresponsible, and then punish her by probably grounding her for a specific period, taking something away, like her cell phone—you get the idea.

That would have made her focus on me and the punishment instead of the act itself. She probably would have stopped listening halfway through my tirade and then resented her punishment. She would have complained to her friends about how horrible I was, and they probably would have validated her feelings. It would not have fixed the situation, just probably made her more careful the next time she wanted to impress her friends and steal my truck.

How to Make Her More Respectful

ONE OF THE things you hear a lot about teenagers is that they have no respect for authority. They don't listen to their teachers, or us for that matter.

My daughter started out doing just that. She would not listen to anything I said, she constantly talked in class, and nothing her teachers said or did brought about any change in her behavior.

Why was she disrespectful?

After observation, I realized the following:

1. She saw her friends doing it, and those friends were labelled as rebels by their

peers. In teenage speak, that means they were cool.
2. She wanted to be seen as cool and get the acceptance of her friends.
3. She did not care about the consequences to herself to achieve this.

My conclusion was that respect has different angles to it: respecting others and respecting themselves. I therefore needed a way to attack the problem on multiple fronts.

I came up with these three rules:

- Respect your child.
- Respect others.
- Respect yourself.

Respect Your Child

As parents, we tend to see our teenagers as children and treat them as such. We have not yet come to terms with their impending adulthood. We therefore don't give much credence to their opinions and put little faith in their judgment. Make sure you put yourself in her shoes and try to see how she could interpret a situation with her limited experience.

Sometimes we may react to something and realize we have overreacted, and as adults, the first impulse is to just walk away and let it go. She's just a kid—she'll get over it, right? Nope, that is the wrong thing to do. Always apologize if you are in the wrong. This will validate her and also pave the way by example for her to admit when she is wrong to you.

I remember, as a child, I wanted a bicycle and my dad promised to get it for me. He got me a bike but not the one I had wanted. I was happy for it, but at twelve years old, I didn't think it was the "cool" bike.

I had an older brother who told me that if I wanted to trade it in, he would pay the difference for me to get the bike I wanted. Of course I jumped at the opportunity but had the good sense to ask my dad first. He said ok, so I then went to my mom. She hit the roof and said I was being selfish and not appreciating the hard work my dad put in to get me the bike.

When I looked at my dad for support, he denied telling me it was ok. He thought I was just a kid and I'd get over it. Nope, decades later, I still remember it with the same amount of betrayal. I never quite forgave him for it, and it clouded our relationship for years afterward. It cheapened him in my eyes, and I could not see him the same after that.

Teenagers are soaking up everything around them, and how you treat them will affect how they see themselves. If you treat them with respect, they will see themselves as someone worthy of respect. They will also respect you. My dad did not treat me with respect. He brushed aside my opinion as the thoughts of a child.

Look at the typical bully at school. Most times, they are disrespected in some way at home. They then perpetuate the action on the outside. If you demonstrate that your child is worthy of respect, there will be less of a need for them to try to get it on the outside.

I remember my daughter's favorite high school teacher. His name was Mr. Goode. She would always come home and tell me about her class with him. He spoke to her as an individual and treated her with respect, and as such, she respected him in return.

Teenagers naturally do not have very good self-esteem, as much as they may pretend otherwise. They have this burning need to belong, to be accepted. We need to do whatever is necessary to build that self-esteem. This will help shield them against the distracting forces outside.

Respect Others

Do you ever find yourself bad-mouthing your neighbors, friends, ex-spouse, or others? As it is for everyone else, the answer is most likely yes. It's human nature, and on a base level, it feels good. However, you have to be very careful how you do it.

You may not realize it, but your kids are watching you closely. They are observing how you handle situations and unconsciously learning from it. Sometimes I would look around and see my daughter watching me intensely. She is looking at my every move and making her own evaluations. How can she hear what you say when she can't hear you over your extremely loud actions?

Case in point, if you were married and undermined your spouse's authority in front of your kids, there would be a strong likelihood that your children would not respect them. If your child's teacher did something that you did not like and you chose to confront the teacher in front of your child and the teacher backed down, yes, you would have demonstrated that you had your child's back; however, the teacher would have lost the respect of your child and probably the ability to effectively teach them anything in the future.

You therefore have to be careful how you handle different situations and how you treat people. If you don't respect other people, how do you expect your child to?

Respect Yourself

As stated above, she is watching you closely, so you also have to watch how you behave. Are you always late? Do you take care of yourself? Are you lazy, or always complaining? If this is you, as the most immediate role model your girl has, what are you teaching her? You are indirectly telling her that this behavior is ok.

Trying to make her more respectful by punishing her will tend to have the opposite effect. She is not too young to recognize hypocrisy. This is a lesson best taught by the subtlety of example, since she has to decide for herself whether or not to respect someone else. With punishment you only get the behavior you want when you are around but once you are not there, she is doing her own thing.

Look for Examples

I always look for examples in real life to demonstrate a point. They can come from anywhere—movies, daily situations, other media, and more. I remember this story I saw on the TV show *60 Minutes* about the opera singer Ryan Speedo Green. He spoke of this one teacher, Elizabeth Hughes, who saw through his anger and treated him with respect. He is now a world-renowned opera singer, and he can still point to her as one of the pivotal people in his life who helped him be the man he is today.

How Not to Alienate Her and to Make Her Listen to You

FOR PARENTS, THIS is an extremely difficult objective to achieve. We can be parent, or we can be friend. Most of us fall into one of those two camps. The parents tend to be more authoritarian, and the friends are the exact opposite.

As we all know, kids seldom open up to "parents." However, they feel more comfortable opening up to "friends." Unfortunately, the "friends" tend to have little control over what the teen does.

How do we navigate both worlds and perform this magical balancing act of being both?

I have discovered three strategies that worked for me. They are as follows:

1. If you want her to listen to you, listen to her.
2. Set boundaries that are fair, and let her be part of the process.
3. Be consistent.

If You Want Her to Listen to You, Listen to Her

I will repeat this point. She learns far more from your actions than from your words. She will even emulate the way you listen, so pay attention when she is speaking. Once you have established a setting where her opinion is respected, she will be more likely to respect what you have to say in return.

By truly listening to my daughter and observing her when we are communicating, I can tell when she is no longer paying attention from the very instant she stops paying attention. This comes in handy during my lectures.

Also, because we, in many cases, discount what our teens have to say, we tend to talk "at" them instead of talking "to" them. Once that occurs, they will stop listening to us.

Set Boundaries That Are Fair, and Let Her Be Part of the Process

I have realized that telling my daughter what to do does not work. Even if what I am saying is correct and she knows it is correct, just the act of me trying to compel her to do anything rubs her the wrong way. Once that is done, she will utilize every strategy at her disposal to undermine whatever I told her to do. She was so good at spotting technicalities that she could have had a future in law.

I would tell her not to fall asleep while watching the TV in the living room since she had a TV in her room. In my mind, if she wanted to sleep, she should go to her room. She would lie down and put the timer on so the TV would turn itself off after an hour and she was free to fall asleep. In her mind, as long as the TV was off, she was not technically sleeping when the TV was on.

I needed to come up with a strategy whereby

my requests were enforced while she had some sense of autonomy. The strategy I developed was to treat everything as a circle. The circle represented the space within which she could do whatever she wanted and not get into any real trouble yet give her that sense of control over her destiny. Once I decided on that course of action, the only decision to be made was the size of the circle. For that, I brought her into the decision-making process.

For example, one of her chores is keeping the house clean. Here, the size of the circle was determining what we considered the house to consist of. As all negotiations go, you have to start throwing everything in, including the things you are willing to give up. I started off with the entire house, including my room, my bathroom, her room, and the guest bathroom. Of course she thought it was not fair that she needed to clean my room and bathroom. I agreed and gave that up. We then had to negotiate about her room and the guest bathroom. Since the guest bathroom was part of the house that everyone had access to, it was considered part of the house. She thought that her room was her domain and that how she kept it was none of my business. I initially forced the issue about her room, but she fought me on it all the time. Eventually, I gave it up since it really was her space.

We now have a compromise, her opinion felt respected, and it is no longer an issue. If she messes up the area we agreed should be kept clean, I can remind her of our bargain and make her clean up on the spot without major repercussions.

Be Consistent

This is where the "parent" comes in. I mentioned this earlier in the book and will mention it again because I cannot stress how important this principle is. Once a course of action is decided upon, it has to be enforced no matter what. For example, if she goes out and we mutually agree on a time she needs to be home by, there must be no deviation. That must be strictly enforced each and every time.

You will be tested time and time again.

Once that occurs, you can refer to the agreement. You can offer to renegotiate the agreement but must insist that there be one hell of a good reason. You tell her that an agreement must never be broken but is open to renegotiation once a suitable reason is given.

Utilizing these strategies has made my daughter feel more in control of the decision-making process. It has taught her that nothing is set in stone and she can actually question and not feel intimidated by authority. Also, you can question authority in a respectful way and with a well-thought-out argument—you may actually be able to elicit change.

How to Get Her to Open Up and Talk to You

WHEN SHE IS with her friends, she can't seem to shut up. Yet when she is with us, the opposite happens. A question about how her day was will be met with "fine." At this juncture, we find ourselves outsiders to her life, our faces pressed against the window, looking in.

This is perfectly normal as she makes her transition into adulthood. She is merely trying to find her own way in the world and become less dependent on Daddy and Mommy.

The problem is, since she is not yet in the place where she is capable of making the best decisions for her long-term well-being, she needs us more than ever. Yet, without a window to her life, we may not always be in a position to help her navigate the hurdles we know she will encounter.

It is therefore critical that we find a way in. We have to be careful how this is accomplished, since anything that is interpreted as us forcing the issue will be met with immediate resistance and tend to be counterproductive.

By trial and error, I have stumbled upon these six strategies that worked for me:

1. See her as a real person.
2. Really listen to her.
3. It's not the end of the world when she makes mistakes.
4. Do not judge.
5. Think from her point of view instead of your own.
6. Know her friends, and get them to like you as much as possible.

See Her as a Real Person
This may sound strange, so it warrants some explanation. Because we gave them life

and grew them up from childhood, we tend to see our kids as just that: our kids. We may not see them the way we see other people.

There are three stages of parenting. When they were too young to understand, we usually just gave orders. As they grew up and could understand but were not yet able to make sensible decisions, we backed off a little but still gave orders. As more time passes, we gradually transition from giving orders to giving advice. I must admit, it's difficult to make the transition from despot to benevolent dictator to advisor.

There is always that overprotective, semi-condescending, and rose-colored-glasses layer we apply to every interaction. Observe yourself when you are talking to a friend or colleague, and compare it to when you are speaking with your child. You will notice subtle differences.

That layer affects how we handle the situations that may occur and how they react. We find ourselves dispensing advice or judgments at every situation instead of hearing what they have to say and responding accordingly.

She will always be your little girl, needing your help and never being quite grown up. However, she is also an individual, with her own opinions and feelings. Sometimes it's difficult to see that and act accordingly.

Really Listen to Her

Because we as parents have lived the teen life before, besides having years of additional life experience, we believe we know more than our kids do. Although this may be true, there is the temptation to discount whatever they say and barely give it credence.

Some of us are more obvious about it and tend to cut our kids off or just tell them, in not necessarily subtle terms, when they are not making any sense. Some of us are more subtle and go through the motions of letting them finish whatever they have to say and just pretend we are actually paying attention. We then go on to make our point, totally disregarding what they said.

First of all, our kids are not stupid. They have their own logic and rationale for the decisions they make. They are also very perceptive, so most times, they can tell whether or not we are truly paying attention to what they say.

If we had a friend who always cut us off when we were making a point, we would eventually just stop speaking with that individual. We would conclude to ourselves that talking to that individual just does not make for a productive conversation. In the same way, if we do that to our teens, we should expect the same result. Also, by not paying attention, we miss an opportunity to peer under the veil of their existence.

From the time she was five years old, whenever my daughter did something wrong, I would begin by asking to hear her side. It did not matter how obviously wrong she was, I always asked her what she had to say. I never said it in an angry tone; I just wanted to elicit what her thought process was. Even when she wrecked the front of my truck, I did that.

I did it earnestly, and the few times that she had a good reason to do what she did, I always acknowledged it. One time, she had an exchange of words with a fellow student and ended up being sent to the principal. Based on my understanding of the events, she was not wrong in what she did since she was standing up for herself. I told her that she was right to feel threatened and that I understood why she did what she did. However, she ended up in the principal's office and everyone got into trouble. So I explained that taking the short-term action had longer-term consequences and that sometimes the immediate response, however tempting and justified it may feel, may not necessarily be the best solution.

By me first acknowledging her thought process instead of blindly telling her how wrong she was, she felt like her opinion was validated and was more comfortable coming to me with issues since she knew that she would always get a fair hearing.

It's Not the End of the World When She Makes Mistakes

I have seen movies where the gangster will send out a hit man to take out the main character. If the hit man fails, he in turn will be killed. Although this is probably the ultimate example of a leader who can motivate his troops to achieve an objective, is it the best way to go about it? I know, it's a hell of a motivating factor, but it doesn't always give the results we may want.

There was a Chinese philosophy called Legalism that was popular starting around 475 BCE, which called for the strict enforcement of laws. It assumes that people are inherently selfish, so the only way to enforce a harmonious society was through force.

There was an emperor called Shi Huangdi around 221 BCE, who was a strong follower of Legalism. He believed that people had to be controlled by a strong ruler with harsh punishments that included body mutilation and death. People took it for a while but ended up forming mini rebellions. There were also several attempts on his life.

One man called Liu Bang, who was faced with death as punishment for an infraction, ended up joining a rebel group. He eventually became the first ruler of the Han Empire. Liu adopted a more tolerant approach to ruling. He adopted the philosophy called Confucianism, which believed in respect for one's parents, justice, beneficence, and strong moral values.

Comparing the two philosophies, Shi's empire lasted around nine years, while the Han dynasty lasted four hundred years. I will let you be the judge. Now, don't you feel a little bit smarter?

I have seen parents, of course to a lesser degree, apply the same principle to their kids. They believe that if they threaten the child with consequences that are severe enough, they will be too afraid to do anything wrong. I believe that works for a while but is not a permanent solution since the desire to obey will only be there when the threat—you—is present.

From my experience, if your teen wants to do anything badly enough, they are going to do it. The problem is, once they have done it, they will endure having their nails pulled one by one before admitting it. Your window to the truth will be closed by fear of consequences. If we don't know what they are doing, how are we supposed to help them fix it and turn it into a teaching moment?

I let my daughter know in no uncertain terms that nothing she does will make me love her less and that whatever she does, I will give her a fair listen and we will get through it together. I make sure that this is not just lip service and live it constantly. Only with that constant reinforcement will it ring true.

Over time, I have seen her actually become more willing to tell me the truth when she does anything wrong.

Most of us take their mistakes personally, almost like a personal betrayal. I mean, we give them love, spend all this cash putting them through school and buying them stuff, and stay up nights when they are sick, and this is how they repay us? That would piss off anyone.

This may cause us to overreact to situations, and that can have disastrous results. They don't make those mistakes to spite us;

they are just being teenagers, exploring their world. Remember, in their world, they come first, and we are a distant second. Fortunately, we have the maturity to understand and accept that, right?

Do Not Judge

Being a single dad, I have always wanted my daughter to have good female role models for her to relate to. There have been teachers and family friends who were female and closer to her age who I have encouraged her to open up to. It never worked. One day, I asked her why she never got closer to any of them. She said that whenever she told them anything, she could tell that they were judging her. Once she felt that, she just clammed up and never allowed herself to get closer.

It is very easy for adults to look at the issues our teens face and judge them by our own standards. Some things they do really seem to be without logic when seen through the lens of experience. We need to bite our tongues and watch our facial expressions and body language.

We need to see the world through their eyes, try to see it from their perspective, and give them a chance to come to their own understanding.

I would tell her not to let her hair go down the drain in the tub because the drain would eventually clog and I would have to snake it. Although she said fine, of course she continued letting her hair go in. I eventually got tired and told her she would have to snake it herself the next time it clogged.

Well it eventually clogged again, and every time she showered, the tub would fill up halfway and there would be a dirty ring around the sides. I told her it needed snaking, and she said she would do it.

Of course she kept putting it off. I did not make her do it. Instead I would do spot checks (no pun intended), and if I saw the ring, I would make her clean it. She ended up cleaning the tub every two days. Did that make her snake it? Of course not! However, I did not relent. I continued making her clean it every two days.

This literally went on for a couple of months. Eventually, she got tired and said she was ready to snake the tub. So I got the drill and snake, and supervised as she did it. You would not believe how much hair came out of that drain. It was a slimy, gooey mess. I did not touch it. I let her do all of the dirty work.

After the drain was clean, she took a shower. After her shower, she came back and told me she couldn't believe how easy it was to clean the tub, since all of the water drained and no ring formed. I congratulated my superhuman willpower not to say something sarcastic.

I could have made her snake the drain a long time ago and made her feel stupid, but I didn't. I let her learn the lesson for herself.

Remember how it was when you were younger? You did stupid things too. If you don't think you did, it may be time for that Alzheimer's checkup.

Think from Her Point of View Instead of Your Own

It doesn't matter how illogical whatever they may say sounds sometimes. In their minds, it makes perfect sense. We need to really make an effort to see things from their point of view before we respond to them. If we don't, our response will do more to alienate instead of endear them to us.

My daughter once told me about a friend of hers who cursed out the teacher because the teacher was picking on her. She said the teacher had it coming because she was always picking on her friend.

Before I responded, I asked her to describe in more detail how the teacher was picking on her friend. It turned out that the friend was always late and talked a lot. The more she told me, the easier it was for me to point out the teacher's perspective as the conversation went along.

Instead of making a blanket statement that the friend was completely out of line, I listened and commented on specific instances. I did not come out in a confrontational way and say that the friend was wrong. I just pointed out the teacher's perspective to each specific incident, showed her a different perspective, and had her draw her own conclusions.

It's easy for us to make a quick assessment of a situation. However, we have the experience. Think of yourself as a manager with a new employee hired to take over some of your responsibilities because you were overworked.

In the beginning, it's faster if you do the work yourself; however, it would be counterproductive to your long-term aims. You would instead sit with the employee, let them go through the process, and make mistakes. You would then correct them and repeat this process as long as necessary for them to take over your responsibilities.

In her mind, her friend was correct, and as a teen, anything rebellious could be considered cool. On a side note, isn't it funny how the word "cool" never went out of style? Slangs come and go, but "cool" is still cool.

I digress, you remember how it used to be, sneaking into your neighbor's yard to tease their dog on a dare, trying to climb to the highest branch on a tree that everyone else is afraid to climb. Now the most rebellious thing we do is to eat spicy food after 8:00 p.m.

Before jumping to a quick judgment, even though you may be right, it is better to patiently help her come to her own realization. That lesson will be infinitely more lasting, in addition to keeping the lines of communication open, and make her more likely to come to you.

Know Her Friends, and Get Them to Like You

If you can pull it off, this is probably the most powerful weapon you can employ in your arsenal. As most parents know, we take a second place to our teens' friends. Many times, their opinions carry more weight than ours. Because of that, we need to figure out a way to get to know their friends. If we can get their friends to like us without compromising on the "parent" aspect of the relationship, we are golden.

With that in mind, I am extremely welcoming and charming to all of her friends. Whenever her friends come over, I come out and joke for a few minutes, ask them about their lives, and just have some light conversation. Note, I do not overstay my welcome. I do it just enough so that they feel welcome. I always ask my daughter how they are doing and sometimes even help them with their homework.

Because of that, I have established pretty decent relationships with her friends, and she feels comfortable bringing them around. Even the friends I may not necessarily approve of, I make them feel welcome. By doing that, there is no reason for her to hide them from me. As they say, keep your friends close . . .

From her friends' perspective, I am not like the other parents, and they actually try to make sure they stay on my good side.

These strategies did not work overnight. It was a very gradual process. My main objective was to make sure that I had a window into her world and make it easy for her to come to me whenever she was having issues. If your teen feels they cannot come to you, they may get the guidance from the wrong sources, and as many of us know, this could have disastrous consequences.

How to Get the Behavior You Want Even When You Are Not There

WE CANNOT BE with our children twenty-four seven; therefore, it is imperative that we figure out a way for them to take our guidance with them.

As I mentioned earlier, some parents try to impart threats so severe with the hope that the teen will be too afraid to do anything wrong. While this may work in the short term, and only in some cases, this is not an effective long-term strategy.

For me, the best strategy is to influence their minds so that they themselves see why something is wrong and understand the dangers of certain courses of actions. They must also understand the causes that will bring about the actions and clearly see the influences for what they are.

I compare both approaches to religion and law. Laws are set for the benefit of society as a whole. Since people are intrinsically selfish, laws may run counter to our base instincts. We therefore have law enforcement to impact consequences to breaking it. Nevertheless, people still break laws all the time. The US has one of the greatest incarceration rates in the world, but crime is still high. This is done for many reasons: survival, peer pressure, greed—and the list goes on. There is no way to prevent the laws from being broken.

Religion, on the other hand, appeals to someone's personal philosophy and value system. There is no religion police. It is practiced by choice.

We therefore need to impart our guidance in a way that it becomes part of their personal philosophy. Only then will we be able to sit back and let the system coast along and merely make adjustments instead of constant course corrections.

These are the strategies that worked for me:

- Explain all of your actions.
- Look for teaching moments.
- Set a good example, and live what you teach.
- Make her part of the decision-making process.

Explain All of Your Actions

When a child is very young and is unable to comprehend language, the only way we could communicate that something should not be done is by physical means. As they grow older and can understand language but do not yet have the ability to fully reason, we just tell them what not to not do in a forceful manner. They may not be able to understand why, but they sure can understand our tone. As they get even older and have increased reasoning abilities, they will begin to resent that ordering approach. At that point, we need to begin utilizing reason and appealing to their sensibilities by explaining why something should not be done.

Sometimes they may do things so infuriating that we forget the prime directive of wanting to grow them up to be responsible adults. We totally lose it and begin yelling all over the place. The problem with this is that all they hear is the yelling and are cowed and then angry at it. Your message will not get through.

As difficult as it may seem, by me holding my temper and explaining, my message always stands a better chance of getting through.

Once, I had grounded my daughter for something, and she said, and I quote, "I want to hate you, but you always tell me why." We both then laughed and hugged, even though I had just punished her.

Look for Teaching Moments

Remember when you were in school and had exams coming up. You knew the schedule all semester, but yet you would wait until the last minute to study for an exam. You were a professional crammer. Unfortunately, even though cramming sometimes worked, you would forget everything you studied within a few days. However, if you had good study habits and took everything in a little at a time when your mind was not stressed, those lessons stayed with you for a much longer time.

Apply that principle to your child. Look for teaching moments. Teaching moments are everywhere—in the movies, on TV, on the street, you name it. Look for the lesson in everything and show her. Her mind will be relaxed, it's very gradual, and you also have a practical example. How cool is that?

Every teen has a friend who does the drugs and alcohol thing. My daughter is no exception. When my daughter started hanging with her and I found out, of course I totally freaked out. However, I did not let her see that I was freaking. I didn't even stop that friend from coming over. In fact, the friend never realized how I felt.

I used her as a test case. I sat my daughter down and told her that her fried looked like she would be in for a very rough life because of her habits. I did not do it in an angry way. I was rather matter-of-fact about it, and I moved on. Whenever the friend did something stupid, I would casually point it out and tie it into the story I had initially told her. It got to the point that she would even tell me when the friend did something stupid. I would make a joke about it and explain what it could lead to. The friend was doing extremely poorly in school and eventually dropped out. When my daughter realized that everything I had predicted was coming true, she did not stop being friends but saw the situation for what it was and got out of it.

Set a Good Example, and Live What You Teach

I stated earlier that your teen learns more from what you do than from what you say. Therefore, you must realize that as a parent, you are never off duty. You must never let your guard down. Your kids are your own personal paparazzi, taking mental pictures of everything you do. If you don't know the song "Cats in the Cradle" by Harry Chapin, I suggest you look it up on YouTube and listen to it with the lyrics streaming on the video. Trust me, you'll get it.

On a side note, as parents, we may want to utilize this tidbit to take a look at ourselves. Take an honest look at your traits, good and bad. Then look at your kids and see how many of those traits are displayed in them. They are a reflection of you, good and bad. One of the reasons I am finishing this book is because of her. I had started it two years ago and told her about it. I got lazy for a while, but I realize that if I don't finish it, she will think it's ok to slack off on things she started.

I have seen my daughter resolve conflicts with her friends using exactly the same approach that I have used with her. At times, she will even tell me that she used some of the things she had seen me do when confronting circumstances as school.

Be cognizant of this fact since it is something we seldom pay attention to.

Make Her Part of the Decision-Making Process

No one likes to be told what to do, and your teen is no exception. Whenever I order my daughter to do anything, even if it is right and makes sense, she will either do it reluctantly or find a way out of it. Remember, they are trying their hardest to be considered adults, and now more than ever, they tend to overcompensate when they think they are being treated as children.

Therefore, I make her part of the decision-making process. For example, if she is going out with friends, we both decide on a reasonable time for her to be home. I let her suggest a time, and then I suggest a time. We then work toward a happy medium.

We also decide on a consequence if our agreement is broken. Never forget this piece. Always agree on a consequence beforehand. That way, neither of you has to be upset either way. As stated previously, you must follow through on the consequence if the deal is broken, no excuses.

How to Help Her Choose Better Friends

AS PARENTS, WE would like our teens to associate themselves with the kids who seem to be going somewhere—the straight A students, the presidents of the debating club, and so on. Unfortunately, to the typical teen, these kids tend not to be exactly popular with their peers. In fact, they avoid them like the plague.

Remember, the teenager's prime directive is to be popular, and if that does not work, then it's just to fit in and to be accepted by their peers. They would do almost anything to this end. If being accepted means doing drugs, having sex, and drinking alcohol, then unfortunately, that's what they will try to do.

I remember, when I was learning to swim, one of the things the instructors did was to take us to the ocean, put us in the middle of a rip current, and tell us to get back to shore. For those of you who do not know what a rip current is, when waves break onto the shore, the water has to find a way back to the ocean. There are natural channels that funnel the water back into the ocean. These funnels take the water back to the ocean as a fast-moving current, and if you get caught up in one, it can pull you out to sea. The more choppy the ocean, the stronger the rip current. This is why it's dangerous to swim when the oceans are choppy. (See what arbitrary facts you can learn while reading a book on some totally unrelated topic?)

The way to get out of a rip current is not to try swimming against it. You have to swim with it and across it. That way, you eventually get out of the channel and can make your way back to shore.

Think of your teen's proclivity to do anything for the acceptance of their peers like a rip current. It's useless to confront it directly and expect you can change its course. You have to employ strategies to go with and across.

Note part of the title of this chapter: "How to Help Her." One fact we must not kid ourselves into believing is that we can choose our kids' friends. The more we try, the more they will resist. In fact, we may inadvertently push them into the waiting arms of the undesirables by our efforts.

The strategies that worked for me are as follows:

- Don't try to choose her friends for her.
- Make friends with her friends.
- Give advice, but do not dictate.
- Keep her friends close.

Don't Try to Choose Her Friends for Her

This statement is obvious, especially in light of the points I made at the beginning of the chapter. Since we have the gift of foresight, we can look at a student and see a kid who has a bright future, while she will only see an unpopular, pimply nerd.

You cannot fight this. Just let it go and move on. Remember, with and across. In fact, the very act of showing that you approve of a kid may permanently brand them as a future minivan-driving conformist to be avoided at all costs.

My daughter once brought home a guy and we sat down and had a great conversation. He knew exactly what he was going to do after high school and had his future mapped out. When I told my daughter that he seemed like a great kid, she said that, yeah, he was just a friend and all of the girls looked at him like their little brother. He was just giving her a ride home, and that was all.

The fact that she was so willing to introduce me to him should have been my first clue to the fact that he was the equivalent of the school mascot. He even drove his parents' minivan, which should have been another clue.

This reminds me of the friend I spoke about in the previous chapter, who swore like a sailor, smoked, and dropped out of high school. How did I handle it? I totally freaked out. Of course, as I said before, I did that internally. I could not show her my reaction. In fact, I embraced that friend just like anyone else she brought home.

That accomplished two objectives. First, it kept her close where I could better see what she was up to. And second, the wall of resistance that my daughter had put up crumbled when she realized that I did not make an executive order forbidding that friend to ever set foot in our house. This flows to my next point.

Make Friends with Her Friends

I actually made friends with the little delinquent she brought home. I would hold her in conversation and ask her about her day and how she was doing. By doing that, I won her approval and, as such, was able to get a foot into my daughter's world.

It may be a jolt to our egos, but there comes a point when what their friends think becomes more important than what we think. Yes, I know, most of the time they don't know what the heck is really going on. However, it still does not change the fact that our opinions have been relegated to the equivalent of commercials between a great sitcom.

Anything we can do to sway their friends' opinions our way will go a long way toward at least becoming a close second.

Passing judgment on our teens' friends would serve no purpose other than to alienate them. One way or another, they would pursue the friendship. It will be done either with or without our knowledge. Personally, I prefer the former.

Your teen is emerging from the cocoon and trying new things. As much as we want to shelter them from the bad and help them avoid the mistakes that seem obvious to us, by not allowing them to explore and make some of those mistakes themselves, they may never learn and will thus be unprepared for the big, bad world into which we cannot follow.

Give Advice, but Do Not Dictate

Remember when your parents told you to do something, you asked them why, and their response was, "Because I said so"? How did that make you feel? Of course it steeled your resolve to either not do it or engage in as much passive resistance as you could get away with. You may have had to wash the dishes, but in silent protest, you were definitely going to drag your feet while doing it, and you also sure as heck would not take the time to scrub every last bit of gunk off that pot. The next time they cooked with that pot, they would inadvertently be having leftovers.

In my youth, I dated a pretty girl with tremendous help from her dad. In truth, I don't think I could have done it without him, the reason being that he did not like me one bit and forbade her to see me. Of course this had the completely opposite effect. I have not forgotten that lesson to this day.

Keep Her Friends Close

If you can establish and maintain some sort of relationship with your teen's friends, as stated above, you will have gained a foothold into their world.

I tried to make my home the coolest in the neighborhood. I created my man cave, and my daughter promptly took it over. At first, I wasn't too happy about it, but then I realized that her friends had started coming over and were hanging out at my house. I had inadvertently created a teen magnet.

If you can show that you neither approve nor disapprove of their friends, being willing to offer advice when asked and refraining from judgment, you create a nonthreatening atmosphere where your teen may feel more comfortable asking for advice they actually listen to.

As parents, we are trying to prevent our kids from making the same mistakes we did. However, they need to make mistakes. It's just part of growing up. You cannot drive a car by watching a video. You also have to experience it directly. Our job is to guide, not live their lives for them.

How to Help Her Make Better Decisions with Boyfriends

THIS IS ONE of the most sensitive areas we will have to deal with. As men, we face particular challenges since we all know exactly how we were at that age. Also, it is difficult to think of our babies as young adults. Because of that, there is the natural inclination to become overprotective.

It's not easy on our little girls either. It may be more difficult to relate to us regarding their feelings toward boys even though we are uniquely qualified. That is a role that, in some instances, may be better filled by another female. However, if they are stuck with us, then that is another challenge to overcome.

Let's face it, most teenage boys are walking hormones with astonishing single-mindedness when it comes to the opposite sex. And we know that! Yet the more we try to tell that to our babies, the more adamant they seem to be about defying our words of wisdom.

The strategies that worked for me are as follows:

- Don't try to choose her boyfriends.
- Give advice, but do not dictate.
- Show her examples from the real world (her friends who make poor choices).
- Swallow the "I told you so" pill.

Don't Try to Choose Her Boyfriends

When I was younger, or should I say young, as I mentioned before, I met this girl. To me, she was the most exquisite individual I had ever seen. There was just one problem: her father hated my guts. However, it actually worked to my advantage since she ended up dating me just to defy him. I am not even sure it would have worked out if he had acted differently. I take that lesson with me always.

Since the females of our species seem to find the bad boys irresistible, and due to young girls not having gained the experience to avoid just that type, there is a strong possibility that's exactly who she will be bringing home.

How we handle that interaction could possibly set the stage for all future occasions when she meets new guys. The first fact you have to accept is that it is going to happen whether you like it or not. The only difference is whether or not she tells you.

Therefore, as much as you would like to freak out, grab the kid by the back of his neck, unceremoniously kick him out the door, and then forbid your daughter under the threat of grounding for life to ever see him again, you must bite your tongue. Even if blood seeps from the corners of your mouth, you have to hold it in. A good acting coach may help.

When she brings him home, she will be watching you closely for any signs of disapproval. Swallow it, and hide the gag reflex. Shake his hand, and look him in the eye. You must master the Jedi stare. That stare must contain the following phrases: I see you, I know your intentions, and you had better not try it here or else I will find you. Looking at some old Clint Eastwood movies may help.

You have to create the atmosphere where she feels like it is ok to bring these guys home. You want to be part of the conversation. If you create an atmosphere where you don't approve of them, she will just stop bringing them over and you will not have the opportunity to offer any guidance.

My daughter once asked me why she should bring the guys over. I asked her, when she met a guy, if she wanted a relationship from him or if she wanted to see him for a couple of weeks and then have him break up with her. Of course she said she wanted a relationship. I then told her that it was not for me to offer judgment since she had to make her own mistakes and learn some of these life lessons for herself. I told her that the guy must know there is someone out there who loves her and is looking out for her. I told her that he must see me, and I see him, and once that occurs, he will treat her with a little more respect.

She actually came back and told me later on that it was true.

There was an episode of the TV show *Family Guy* where this guy Quagmire, who was the man whore of the show, was giving advice to a young man. He told the guy that the first question he should ask a girl is what type of relationship she had with her dad. If she said the relationship was good, then walk away. My daughter and I had a good laugh about it afterward.

Remember, you always want to be part of the conversation; therefore, you must never be too hasty and pass judgment.

Give Advice, but Do Not Dictate

Like I said before, we know exactly where the road is leading when she meets some guys. With that, there is the temptation to step in and tell her what she needs to do. Remember, that flower is in the process of blooming, and our task is to provide an atmosphere where it can bloom properly. Grabbing hold of the petals and manually opening them may cause damage and sabotage the actual task we are trying to accomplish.

Teenagers are trying to find themselves and many times resent and oftentimes rebel against our best efforts to guide them properly. Therefore, hold your tongue, create open dialogue, and wait for her to ask questions. Once that happens, you will be in a much better position to be heard. No one likes a know-it-all, and that is exactly how you will come across if you try to offer unsolicited opinions.

Of course you have to create an atmosphere where she feels comfortable to open up. One of my daughter's favorite lines is that she feels like someone is judging her. Once she gets that feeling, she shuts down. I have always been mindful of how I come across since then.

Show Her Examples from the Real World (Her Friends Who Make Poor Choices)

This is similar to looking for teaching moments, as I mentioned in a previous chapter, even though you cannot dictate. Also, to some extent, give them some degree of freedom to make their own mistakes. I stress "to some extent." Note, that doesn't mean she can go out all night. There must be boundaries. Now, that doesn't mean there is nothing you can do to be proactive. You just have to be subtle.

Look up teen romantic comedies. You will find an abundant supply of teaching examples there.

I was able to size up virtually every guy she brought into the house, and I am reasonably confident you can too.

I would ask how the date went, and if I saw anything suspicious in his behavior, I would comment on it and tell her what I thought it meant and what to look out for in the future. Notice I did not say anything about whether or not she should stay with the individual. I just offered my opinion on what certain behaviors could mean.

I wanted her to be cognizant of what the signs meant so she would not be surprised when anything occurred. When more and more of my predictions came to pass, she came to me more frequently for advice. Not once did I suggest she break anything off. I just answered the questions asked.

Swallow the "I Told You So" Pill

Of course, all good things may come to an end. It is highly unlikely any of the guys she brings home will end up being your son-in-law; therefore, there will be many broken hearts that will occur along the way. Since we have the benefit of experience, we tend to have a pretty good idea how most of her relationships will end.

There is the temptation to put on that smug smile and say the famous words "I told you so." Again, you must bite your tongue. Remember, you want to keep the dialogue open, and how you handle the first one will dictate your future interactions.

You want to build her self-esteem and her BS radar so she can go out into the world properly equipped to spot trouble sooner.

How to Make Her Want to Progress and Try in School

NOT MANY OF us are blessed with the daughter who has any aspiration beyond hanging at the mall the next weekend with friends, social media, and boys. As cool as that may sound, we know a little more than that is required for success in today's world.

My daughter was no exception. These topics seemed to fill her days. Schoolwork was just the chore to get out of the way so she could get to the more important things in life, stated above.

The strategies I came up with for this were as follows:

- Expose her to appropriate role models.
- Set a good example.
- Help her find what she really wants. (They think short term.)
- Show her what her future would look like without an education, and give real-world examples. (The world is your teacher and is full of examples.)

Expose Her to Appropriate Role Models

Teenagers are notorious for following the crowd. This is partially due to their quest of self-discovery and their need to belong. Instead of getting angry at her lack of interest in what I deemed important, I decided to study her actions and see if I could discern any patterns. I would pay attention to what she liked on social media and the topics she and her friends considered interesting.

When she was younger, like many of her peers, she passed through the Hannah Montana phase and would sometimes dress like her. As she got older, her tastes changed and became more sophisticated. Instead of just blindly following what her idols did on screen, she became part of the paparazzi culture. She would follow what they did off screen as well. I figured that I could use that to my advantage.

Not all teen idols have exactly perfect backgrounds. There was a time when she admired Lindsay Lohan. Whenever there was an incident in the news, I would bring it up in conversation—not in an accusing way, of course, because that would have immediately put her on her guard. I would casually bring up the incident and ask her what she thought. This had the effect of my recognizing her right to an opinion in addition to providing some subtle validation.

Most times, she would give me an earful about Lindsay losing her way, and I would ever so slightly ask her how she imagined her parents must be to have a child grow up with so many issues. What she said totally floored me, and for a second, the heavens opened up and angels rained down. She said that Lindsay did not have any boundaries. Can you believe it? This actually came up her esophagus, into her mouth, and out into the world.

We then had a discussion about the need for boundaries, and all I did was ask the questions about what would happen if a child did not have any boundaries. I was even able to point out some of her friends and ask her what she thought their future would be like since they seemed to be able to go out all night and performed horribly in school.

I then thought about appropriate role models. Finding appropriate role models is not that simple. They had to be people she could relate to and incentivize her to action. One of the role models I chose was a guy called Randy Pausch. Randy got an undergraduate degree at Brown University and a PhD from Carnegie Mellon. He went on to write five books and was listed as one of the world's top one hundred most influential people.

Randy may sound like the most unlikely candidate for a teenage girl's role model. However, the thing is, they both went to the same high school. Yep, Randy actually went to the same high school that she did. I used that as my opener, and instead of beating her over the head about it, I would just drop subtle hints about him from time to time and let her curiosity take over.

Set a Good Example

As I mentioned before, sometimes I would catch her watching me intensely when she thought I wasn't looking. Thinking about this made me realize that she was actually observing me and looking at how I dealt with various situations. That realization made me become very conscious of how I dealt with the world when I was under her gaze.

Some of us are the type of parents who ascribe to the theory "Do as I say but not as I do." Again, the song "Cats in the Cradle" by Harry Chapin comes to mind.

How do we expect them to be patient if we fly off the handle for every little thing? How do we expect them to be reliable if we make promises to them and constantly break them? How do we expect them to respect us if we take them for granted and do not give them the appropriate respect?

For single dads, this takes on a particular significance. We are the benchmark upon which men are going to be judged. Have you ever heard the saying that girls grow up to date their fathers? I keep that in mind all the time.

We may think, she is just a kid and I am a grown man, so I can do whatever I want. That is not a very good idea. Nothing we do goes unnoticed. Treat your relationship with her as you would any relationship, because that's exactly what it is: a relationship. Whenever I go out, I tell her where I am going and when I expect to be back. If we have a disagreement and I turn out to be wrong, I will own up to it and apologize. I even keep my room tidy.

Help Her Find What She Really Wants (They Think Short Term)

Teenagers are notorious for thinking short term. Girls are a little ahead of the curve when compared to boys, but not by much. My daughter was no exception. As a young teenager, she could not envision life beyond high school. Life was her friends and boys. Looking deeper, it was really about fitting in since that's what everyone was doing.

Getting her to shift her focus was not the easiest task in the world. It's like the swimming story I mentioned earlier. It's useless to fight a current. Remember the best way is to go with and across it until you get out of it. I decided to apply that principle. I did not try to go against her penchant for hanging on to her friends and talking about boys all day long. That would have been trying to go against the current and probably resulted in my drowning in her resistance. Get it?

As with everything else, if you want her to do something, it is never a good idea to approach the subject directly. Remember, you are not cool. You are just an old fart cramping her style, and you don't know anything.

It's easier to figure out a way to have the topic develop naturally, and if you can make it her idea, even better. This is where our listening skills become important. Resist the urge to lecture her about how she is wasting her time and should be looking toward the future. Her eyes would start to glaze over, and she would mentally tune into another station.

One thing I knew about my daughter was her love of talking. So I would engage her in conversation where she did most of the talking. The key to make this work is to withhold judgment no matter what she says. If she felt like I was judging her, she would shut up faster than a blunt would last at a Bob Marley concert. I know this (not about the blunt) because she once told me that she did not talk to some adults because she felt like they were judging her. See, sometimes listening pays off.

I would ask her how her friends were doing, not just in school but generally. Once she was loosened up, we played the imagination game of "If we won the lottery, what would we do?"—not just with the money but with the free time the money allowed her to have.

I believe a lot of us, in fact the majority of us, work for the money to help us live the life we want. We never look at it the other way around: that work is part of life, and if we can find out what it is we truly enjoy, then those hours spent working will not be wasted hours. Face it, for now, we consider working doing chores.

Helping my daughter find out her true passions as early as possible was me giving her some insight into herself and figure out what it is she really wanted to do with the time between wake and sleep as an adult.

I never told her what the true purpose of these discussions was. I just wanted her to truly look at herself and figure herself out. That way, when the time came, I reminded her about those conversations and what she had said.

Her passion is children. She is generally irresponsible with everything else, but when it comes to children, a different side takes over. I remember we were taking care of a friend's five-year-old daughter. My daughter was around twelve at the time. I took them to a fast-food restaurant called Cheeburger Cheeburger. (Nope, I didn't make this up.)

The little girl had a peanut allergy, which I knew about but was absentminded about it. When the waitress came out and gave us the menu, I told them they could have whatever they wanted. My daughter stopped the waitress and started scanning the menu. She told the waitress about the peanut allergy and checked the ingredients of anything the little girl wanted, including asking about cross contamination.

Can you believe it? At twelve years old, she showed more responsibility than I did. I felt like a total idiot. I was sure to let her know how proud of her I was and never forgot that incident.

People discover new things about themselves all the time; therefore, it would not be realistic for you to expect your daughter to know everything about herself and make the right decision for the rest of her life. The point is to teach her the art of self-examination and utilize those skills throughout her life.

Show Her What Her Future Would Look Like without an Education, and Give Real-World Examples (The World Is Your Teacher and Is Full of Examples)

I once read a book called *Change Anything: The New Science of Personal Success*, written by Kerry Patterson, Joseph Grenny, David Maxfield, Ron McMillan, and Al Switzler. Like the title says, it describes strategies to help people make meaningful changes in their lives. I strongly recommend it, by the way.

One of the things outlined in the book was to visit your default future. What that means is to look at your present state and imagine what your future would be like if you kept doing what you are doing now. Not just a quick glance, but imagine it in vivid detail and play it over and over in your mind. For most people dissatisfied with their present condition, this would be a rude awakening since we tend to put off anything that looks even a little painful even though it's something we should be doing.

Of course, with my daughter, I could not do that directly. Instead I looked at her friends, and for the ones I knew were heading down the wrong path, I would ask her what she thought of them and where she thought they would be in ten years. Invariably, she would hit the nail on the head and knew full well that their lives were headed nowhere. You see, it is easier to examine and judge other people. Its self-examination that's hard.

I never applied the analogy to her because I knew it would make her defensive. I wouldn't just look at her friends. I would also look at the characters in the teen movies she watched and play the same game with her. I let her figure it out for herself.

There is a 1983 movie called *WarGames*, where this government computer was getting ready to launch all nuclear missiles at Russia because it thought the US was under attack. The computer guys were unable to disable the launch, so they taught the computer the game tic-tac-toe.

I'm not sure how much you know about the game, but if you and your opponent both know the tricks, every game will end in a draw.

Their aim was to see if the computer would quickly learn the game and determine that games where there can be no winner are not worth playing and to tie it to the missile launch and stop. Of course, the computer got it and disaster was averted, but you get my point.

One of the rules to writing a great movie script is to show and not tell. Never tell the audience about a character; just show them the character's actions and let them figure it out for themselves. It also works in real life. Telling your daughter not to do something will not have as great an effect as showing her the consequences of a course of action and letting her figure it out for herself.

How to Get Her to Do Her Chores

THIS HAS BEEN one of my biggest challenges, as I am sure it has been for you. Many of the teenagers I've seen are notoriously lazy. I take that back, lazy may not be the best choice of words. Let's face it, if there is something they really want to do, they can show remarkable persistence and diligence. For example, squeezing us for money to go to the movies or buying the latest outfit. The more appropriate term may be "unmotivated."

I once read a book about the best CEOs, which detailed the ones who can get the best out of their people. When you are running an organization, your success is dependent on getting the best out of other people. The best CEOs had a knack for motivating their employees and getting the best out of them.

Their secret was to get their employees to buy into the mission of the organization, to elevate their function to more than just a job. That way, each employee saw their role as more than a job, rather as a contribution to the ultimate goal.

Well, my friend, you are the CEO of your household, and your function is to motivate your direct reports. I know motivating a teenage girl about doing chores is not exactly as easy as parking a three-wheeler with a kickstand, but it is possible.

To be honest, I have not been able to fully conquer this aspect of rearing, although it has gotten progressively less difficult as she's gotten older. I will share with you some of the strategies that have worked for me. They are as follows:

- Why is she doing chores? (Lesson)
- Let her be part of the decision-making process.

- Give her responsibilities.
- They're not chores. It's a job.
- Compromise.

Why Is She Doing Chores? (Lesson)

Since I am trying to mold her into the adult I want her to be (see mission statement), my first approach was to make sure she understood why she needed to perform chores. I explained to her that this was also her home and will probably belong to her after I am gone. As such, I want to ensure it is in the best condition possible for her to take over. I drew an analogy to her coveted cell phone. I told her that in order to be able to keep her phone for a long time, she had to take care of it. Like her phone, the house needed care.

I explained that I also had chores, such as cutting the grass, taking out the trash, and fixing things that needed fixing. I did not think that they were fun either, but they were necessary. We both had to do our part to ensure our home is well taken care of, and since I was doing my chores, I expected her to do hers as well.

Let Her Be Part of the Decision-Making Process

When she was younger, she was highly opinionated. Wait a minute, she still is. I guess some things never change. What I had learned was that when I let her have her way, she almost always followed through on what she had decided to do.

I decided to use that as she got older. When the time came to get the chores done, I created a list and let her decide when she could reasonably get each one accomplished. I determined the chores, but I let her set the schedule. Most chores, such as cleaning the bathroom and mopping the floor, had to be done weekly. However, for those other chores requiring a great frequency, such as emptying the dishwasher and keeping surfaces tidy, I let her decide within what time frame they needed to be done. For example, once the dishwasher was clean, it needed to be emptied within twenty-four hours.

The critical thing is, never let this slip. As is human nature, she would try to extend the time and not always get her stuff done on time. I would without fail pull her up on those times and remind her of our agreement. I also left the door open to renegotiate as long as she could give me a good enough reason. This had the effect of honing her negotiation skills and showing her the proper way to question authority.

As she got older, to my annoyance, she would question everything, such as why her curfew was set for a specific time. However, this was the way I had raised her, so I never gave her the answer "because I said so," no matter how much I was tempted to do so.

Give Her Responsibilities

You can call a garbage collector a trash man, or you can call him a sanitary engineer. They both mean the same thing, but one seems a bit more elevated than the other. If you received a bottle of wine in a brown paper bag, and another time you received the same wine in an antique-style box with the name of the wine engraved on it, which would taste better? Coke in a can or a glass bottle also comes to mind.

The point is, it's all about the packaging. In our superficial culture, perception is reality. We all go for what is flashy, completely ignoring the substance, which is why we have the politicians we do, but that's another story. Why should our little ladies be any different? Our home is just a microcosm of society as a whole, so I decided to use that theory when it came to chores.

Let's not call them chores. They are responsibilities. "Responsibilities" sounds more grown up, don't you think? Kids have chores; adults have responsibilities.

They're Not Chores. It's a Job

Let's face it, using all of those psychological strategies can only get you so far. We are dealing with teenage girls, after all. Therefore, we need to have many tricks up our sleeves besides going totally psycho and yelling at her to get it done that instant!

Once again, I refer to my mission statement. Since I am preparing her for adulthood, I wanted her to have the adult experience.

With that in mind, I am about to share with you my ultimate strategy. I wanted to find one of her main motivators to action. The two main motivators were having her friends like her and being able to have nice things. Since there is nothing about chores that can make your friends like you, I focused on her love for perfume, clothes, costume jewelry, etcetera. With that in mind, I gave her a job.

Yep, that's right. I gave her a job. We came up with the job description, which was essentially her chores, oops, I mean responsibilities list, and here is the secret: each item on the list had a value. The total value of the list came up to what her allowance was for the week. Each item had to get done within the allotted time and with the expected quality for her to be paid. I wasn't totally mean if it didn't get done. The value would be reduced the more she breached her deadline. If the deadline was missed by more than two days, then it was taken away.

Every weekend, we would go through the list together and determine what was done from what wasn't. If something didn't get done, I saved money, and I was very happy to point out that fact.

You may ask the question, what if she already has a job? Well since she is now older, I did experience that issue. What I did was start charging her when something wasn't done. Yep, that's right, she needed to pay me when she didn't do something.

The funny thing is, when I was giving her money, the effect wasn't as strong as when she was paying me. She has grown up to be an amazing tightwad, and having to hand over money is like giving up her firstborn. So this has been a pretty effective strategy for me.

Compromise

Part of having them learn to be an adult is allowing them the ability to make their own mistakes. No one has ever gotten things right the first time. It's easy for us to tell them what to do and expect it to be done. However, with that approach, personal growth is limited. We tend to internalize the lessons we learn on our own much better than the lessons taught to us by others. Remember the *WarGames* movie.

With that in mind, I allowed her to have a space that was all her own and she could do with as she pleased. That space was her room. When she was younger, I was very strict on how the room needed to be kept. Remembering my childhood, I was determined to do the exact opposite of whatever my parents forced me to do.

Therefore, if I had maintained that control over her room, thinking it would teach her cleanliness, we know how that would have ended.

I divided the house into three areas: her space, my space, and common space. The common space had to be kept clean, and we could do whatever we pleased with our respective spaces. Of course I knew that I needed her to live up to whatever standard I expected of her; therefore, my room was always kept clean.

I have said it before and will repeat it as often as necessary: she is looking at you and making decisions on whether or not you are credible, whether or not you are worthy to be listened to. Therefore, you must always walk the talk.

What I noticed was that her room started off being completely messy all the time. I bit my lip and said nothing, all the while keeping my room clean. Over time, it became less crazy. Now it will be messed up for a few days and then she will tell me that she can't function in that much disorder and will clean it up on her own. She is not there yet, but I am seeing progress.

Like I stated at the beginning of the chapter, these were not 100 percent effective, but they did help a significant amount in getting her to get things done.

How Not to Let Her Be Affected by Peer Pressure

WHEN SHE WAS much younger, I remember looking at the news, more specifically teen statistics. I saw the rates of accidents teens got into, teen pregnancies, drugs, alcohol, and just about everything bad that happens to teens. I realized that most of that was caused by peer pressure.

Remember, one of our teens' greatest needs is to belong. They would do almost anything to fit in. If you remember back in the day—of course some of us would have to remember further back than others, but try anyway—we were exactly the same. We all wanted to be cool, or whatever the slang was back then. I think "cool" still applies, however. Let's face it, cool is forever.

While we were growing up, the consideration of peer pressure was not even considered part of the equation in raising a child. Our parents just told us what to do and we did it. When we wanted to follow the crowd, we did and just didn't let our parents know. Of course, the kind of trouble we got into back then was very different from the kinds of trouble kids get into these days.

The thing about peer pressure is that we will never be around to see it happen. It's one of those intangibles. A lot of times, they don't even know when it's happening. Also, when they are going with the crowd, it's often something they shouldn't be doing anyway, and confiding in us is almost analogous to the prison snitch complaining to the guards. I have not yet heard of a teen getting "shanked," but you get my point. They don't know it is happening, and they won't be telling us anyway.

We therefore have to be proactive in this

area. Some of the strategies that worked for me are as follows:

- Encourage education.
- Praise her.
- Build her self-esteem.
- Give her a sense of self.

Encourage Education

The fact that most teens don't even realize when they are being affected by peer pressure makes them more susceptible to it. I therefore made it my business to ensure she understood what the concept was all about. As I said before, lessons are everywhere. I looked for examples in movies, real life, and anywhere else I could find it.

Teen movies are a great source of that type of information since a lot of them—when they are not pandering to the teen need of seeing pretty people who glitter in the sun—actually try to impart lessons. Therefore, don't entirely discount them as mindless drivel. If you are ever fortunate enough to be allowed a glimpse into her world by going to see a movie together,

I recommend going to see a teen movie. You will get points for trying to see things from her point of view, plus you can help her to see the movie in a different light by pointing out the lessons you find.

Of course you have to be extremely careful how you point out these lessons because there is the risk of sounding preachy or judgmental, since that could ruin the effect you are going for and seriously jeopardize your chances of a repeat performance. Timing is important. No one likes anyone who talks nonstop during the movie. There will be plenty of time afterward.

On the way home, you can get her take on it first, which will probably entail a description of the cute lead actor and the female lead's outfits. Make sure you do not roll your eyes or betray any symptom of disinterest. Give her your undivided attention, and show genuine interest in her opinions. If you do that, she will be more likely to show interest in yours. Remember, she is learning even more from what you do than from what you actually say. Do the right things and what you say will more likely be positively received.

In a subtle way, this will have the effect of showing her that her opinion counts. It helps validate her as a human being. Also, you may not realize it, but this also has the dynamics of a date—of course not in the creepy sense, but demonstrating to her that anyone she goes on a date with has to pay her the appropriate attention and respect her opinions. You are the benchmark upon which all men will be measured. Make sure the standard is as high as you can make it.

Praise Her

Like most parents, I sometimes feel like she cannot do anything right. I remember reading somewhere, someone said that you can do one hundred things well but if you make one mistake, that's all anyone will remember. That is definitely true when it comes to our kids.

I have to remind myself of this all the time. I used to drive a stick shift, and sometimes I would find myself in fifth gear, cruising on the highway, and when I tried to remember when I had made the gear shifts from one to five, a lot of times I couldn't remember.

Take a look at that in your own life. Can you remember exactly how you brushed your teeth this morning or how you put your socks on? If, however, you stubbed your toe on your way to the bathroom, I am pretty sure you would remember that for a while. The harder you stubbed it, the longer you would remember it.

This is not necessarily a bad thing. Your brain is an amazing organ. In an effort to make things as efficient as possible so we can get on with the task of living, it tries to automate as much as it possibly can. If something is done repeatedly, then that process is standardized so we no longer think about it. This was outlined in a book called *Thinking, Fast and Slow* by Daniel Kahneman, another one I recommend. However, once something out of the ordinary happens, it creates a blip in the otherwise-flat line of our existence.

When you live with someone for a while, there is the risk of falling into this. The consideration that is shown, if done frequently, is eventually taken for granted. As long as she does what she is supposed to do, it falls into our standard processes and we may no longer see and recognize it. However, if anything happens contra to that, such as nonperformance of chores or doing something else to get into trouble, since we no longer remember the good things, we tend to zero in on that negative incident.

The result is, she thinks she does nothing right. Even though she doesn't show it, what you think of her means more than you will ever know. It's just not cool to show it. Yes I said "cool."

We need to never take the good things for granted. Recognize the little things, and make sure you tell her. The old saying that you get more with honey than with vinegar has stood the test of time and is one of the truths of human nature. She craves your approval, so give it. On a side note, this holds true for all relationships.

Build Her Self-Esteem

Low self-esteem is one of the factors that make someone seek validation elsewhere. This affects adults as well as children. What's interesting is that even the cool kids have self-esteem issues unless they are a psychopath. Hopefully that's not your little girl; otherwise, you have real problems. It is therefore a safe assumption that our girls have it. It's like an infectious disease. The most dangerous carriers are the mass media, displaying ideals that no one can live up to, friends, and the ultimate carrier, us.

Yes, that is entirely accurate: the worst carrier is us. We can devastate her with our words, a glance, or even by our very actions. I remember, once, my daughter had lost a violin. I won't go into the detail of how she lost it, but it was done in a really thoughtless fashion. I was so upset that I just avoided her completely for a while. I needed to get over my anger, and that was the only way I knew how.

I only realized later that my reaction had completely devastated her. It wasn't like I had gotten angry; it was like I had rejected her. She did not take that well and became very withdrawn. Once I realized it, I had a long talk with her and worked it out.

Another time, I allowed her to have a get-together at home but told her specifically to be careful who she invited. Of course her desire to be popular made her have an open-door policy. The result was that someone stole my PlayStation from the basement.

I learned from my mistake years earlier and made it a teaching moment. The benefit was that she was so relieved I had not totally freaked out that I had her undivided attention. We talked about why she needed to have the party in the first place, which was of course to be popular and accepted. We also talked about who her real friends were. She acknowledged that her real friends would never have done that and, to some extent, being popular was just an illusion. I never would have gotten that far if I had reacted instead of acted.

Although this did not exactly build her self-esteem, it made her realize it's more important to surround yourself with people who love you than to try to seek out the blind admiration of others.

Give Her a Sense of Self

If you ask the average person who they are, one of the most common answers you will get is what they do for a living. Our society is so externally focused that we have come to define ourselves in exactly those terms.

We are bombarded every day with useless information and a myriad of distractions. There are movies, the internet, email, social media, and the list goes on. We have managed to fill most of our waking hours almost entirely with consuming this stimuli, to the point where we are no longer comfortable with silence and looking inward.

Don't take my word for it. I would like you to perform an experiment. Any time there is a line of people waiting to do anything, take a look and see how long it takes for someone to whip out their cell phone. Look at the train, bus, or any other public transportation and see how many people have their cell phones out, looking at nothing in particular. We have become a culture that needs to fill every instant of every day with some form of external entertainment. We have become vessels of passive consumption.

I remember this episode of *Family Guy* when their TV broke and they had to find other ways to entertain themselves. Peter took the family hiking, and they participated in a lot of outdoor activities. They became healthier and happier. When the TV was fixed, they went back to being vegetables.

Teenagers are the biggest victims of this phenomenon, being more impressionable than most, and the result is someone who defines themselves by whatever society dictates. Society gets to say what is cool and what isn't. There could be benefits to this; however, the media—being the self-serving prostitute to profits and ratings—will mainly idolize whatever serves that end.

As a result, they tend to display whatever garners the most attention, which is not always positive. I once read about a famous man, whose name I cannot remember. He was asked how he was able to remain humble despite his great fame. He replied that even though he was able to attract great crowds now, when he died, his funeral would probably be twice as large. The point is that people tend to be more attracted to sensationalism. Look at the crowd that gathers at the scene of any accident.

To combat this, we need to ensure our girls have a strong sense of self and avoid this external definition so many of us fall victim to. The way to do this is to help her become self-aware. This is no easy task, as even many adults are not self-aware.

This is accomplished by helping them observe themselves as they go through their days. Observe how they react to different circumstances, and try to understand the reasons for their actions. For example, my daughter used to like putting on a ton of makeup and enough perfume to suffocate a fish while it was underwater. I asked her why she did it. Note, I did not offer an opinion. I merely asked her why she did it. She initially said it was because she liked it, but on closer examination, it turned out to be because her friends were doing it and she thought that was what the boys liked.

I showed her that boys, on a subconscious level, can tell when someone is trying too hard, the result being that they will respect her less and it will make her appear more desperate—both things she definitely did not want. I did this in many other subtle ways. By asking why she did things and without showing any judgment, she gradually started questioning things herself.

No one ever comes completely out of the desire to please others, and my daughter is no exception. This is therefore a lifelong work in progress. However, I was able to put her on the path with a good foundation.

How to Get Her to Be More Responsible

ONE OF THE greatest symbols of adulthood is to be responsible. A lot of us only learn that lesson by trial and error, when we are suddenly thrust out into the unsympathetic world on our own. When we were at home, under the safe protection of our parents, that lesson never seemed to strike home, as much as they may have tried. We remain irresponsible until the very last second—in other words, when we have no choice.

History somehow repeats itself when we have kids. We expect that it will be different; however, it never is. They turn out just as irresponsible as we were. We are frustrated by the fact that we have to micromanage everything they do. Every chore she is given, she does halfway. We have to tell her to do everything that needs to be done, and she never shows some initiative by doing something that needs to be done without being asked to do it. In my case, for example, I would ask her to wash the dishes in the sink or put them into the dishwasher. She would clear the sink but leave the residual food scraps in the sink. If I had any hair left, I would have been tempted to pull them out.

I wanted so desperately for her to be like a peer, someone to share responsibilities with instead of having to play the role of dictator, someone who understood. Every time I had to tell her to do something, I got a little annoyed, and the more times I had to tell her, the more annoyed I became. At those times, I was extremely tempted to react. Honestly, sometimes I did.

As discussed in previous chapters, yelling only worked in the short term. At those times, I would have to remind myself of my mission statement: **I want my daughter to be a confident, honest, and responsible adult, someone who has a strong sense of self, is capable of handling failures without self-doubt, and believes she can accomplish anything.**

I recognized that she was a work in progress and that I had a few more "seasoning" years on her. With that understanding, I was able to get my emotions under control and not totally freak out most of the time.

Some of the strategies that worked for me are as follows:

- Identify her motivating factors.
- Show her the big picture.
- Lead by example.
- Give her responsibilities, not tasks.
- Hold her accountable.

Identify Her Motivating Factors

There was a time when she would always break her cell phone. It didn't matter how much I yelled about it, she would never take proper care of it. One day, she finally got a smartphone. She was so excited. However, I kept the old "pay as you go" phone and told her that anytime she broke the smartphone, I would not replace it. She would instead go back to the old phone. Miraculously, she never damaged that smartphone.

I then realized she was capable of responsible thinking; she just didn't always have the proper motivation. I needed to figure out how to make that work to my advantage. I needed to figure out what her motivating factors were. After some thought, I realized her motivating factors were her peers and boys. Everything that flowed was some variation on that theme.

If she wanted an iPhone, it was because her friends either had it or thought it was cool. If she wanted a new outfit, it was because either her friends thought it was cool or the boys would like it. It was pretty simplistic once I thought about it. Therefore, as long as I could involve a consequence that would involve her motivating factors, I would be ok.

Looking at things from my perspective all those years was completely wrong and only led to personal frustration. To be fair, I was not always able to relate consequences to her motivating factors, but in those instances that I could, I milked it to the maximum.

Show Her the Big Picture

When our girls were very young and did not yet have the ability to understand concepts, we had to use the "because I said so" approach. However, as they got older, that approach needed to be modified. As she matures and gradually becomes a young woman, she will expect to be treated as such. Therefore, giving orders without explanation is a guaranteed recipe for disaster. You can almost be sure your orders will be ignored.

As my daughter got older, one of her pet peeves was feeling like she was being treated as a child. As far as she was concerned, if you respected her, she would respect you. If she felt like I was talking down to her, she would resist as far as technically possible. She would always try to find some technical loophole to disobey an order if she felt disrespected.

I must admit, it was an adjustment for me,

but once I realized the new status quo, I was able to make it work. In addition, tasks are not objective driven from the point of view of the person doing it. It is just a chore. No one is ever motivated by a task, since either they don't see the reason behind it or there is no buy-in to why it is being done.

I realized that I had to either get her buy-in or at least ensure she understood the reason behind doing anything I asked her to. Therefore, every time I asked her to do something, I would ask her if she knew why I was asking her to do it. Whenever she said no, I would take the time to explain it.

I would like to say that things worked smoothly after that, but hey, we are dealing with teenagers, after all. There were ups and downs, but her resistance never escalated to outright rebellion. I was ok with that.

Understand that this will not work unless the foundation has been laid. If you do not start recognizing her budding maturity and keep seeing her as a ten-year-old who needs constant direction, this is destined to fail.

Lead by Example

For a second, close your eyes and picture that you're married. Imagine opening your eyes one day and not feeling the motivation to do anything. We all have those days, and it's perfectly natural. We are human, after all.

Imagine if you were married and telling your wife that you would like to stay in bed all day, she would have to take the kids to soccer practice, and you are just not in the mood to fix that faucet that has been leaking for a while. Imagine her frustration and eventual silent resentment. Now open your eyes and ask yourself how many nights you would be sleeping on the sofa before she eventually left you.

Bottom line is that you have to pull your weight in the relationship. It must never be one-sided. We all understand and respond to fairness. If something is determined as unfair, then don't expect cooperation.

Now look at your daughter. She is not a little girl anymore. Now that she is older, she expects to be treated as the young lady she is. Never forget that. She is evaluating not just what you say but what you do as well.

For example, at this very moment, it has been a few months since I started this book. What's worse is that she knows it. I did not realize it until we were chatting one day, and out of the blue, she asked me how the book was going. I knew that I had put it on the back burner for a few months. I told her that I was waiting until the spirit took me. She just looked at me and said, "Uh-huh."

I knew immediately that was the wrong thing to say. My own actions just gave her a reason that procrastination was ok. It also made me look at myself, and I saw that I actually do tend to procrastinate on a lot of things.

That being the case, how could I then insist on perfection from her? The good thing is that I started paying closer attention to how I lived and tried as best I could to set a better example. Of course I got off my butt and resumed the book.

When you ask her to do something, she is making an evaluation within her budding sense of judgment. Since she is not yet seeing the larger picture, there is a natural inclination for resistance. You can teach far more by what you do than by what you say.

Give Her Responsibilities, Not Tasks

Since she is now coming of age and figuring out who she is, the old tried-and-true method of "because I said so" no longer flies. We now have to appeal to her intellect. This is borne out by the fact of her questioning everything we say, and in some instances rebelling. This is perfectly normal, so don't get frustrated.

Remember, we are preparing her for adulthood, and with that in mind, we have to modify how we approach a situation. Children are task driven, and adults are objective driven. She must therefore be given objectives to achieve instead of just tasks.

I thought about all the things that needed to get done around the house and tried to figure out how to phrase the chores as responsibilities instead of tasks.

Since it was just the two of us, the responsibilities needed to be divided equitably. She was responsible for maintaining the interior of the house, and I was responsible for taking out the trash, fixing anything that needed fixing, and maintaining the exterior of the house.

We came up with a list of things that needed doing to ensure the objective of maintaining the interior was achieved. I explained to her that it was her responsibility and that I needed her help in ensuring the larger objective of maintaining the entire house was achieved.

There was one time that she had a friend stay over for a while. Since the friend was not aware of how we did things, I told my daughter that it was her responsibility to make sure her friend abided by the overarching rule of maintaining the household. I explained to her that I was executive management making the strategic decisions, and she was management ensuring the goals were met, and to consider her friend as an employee she was responsible for.

It was easier to sell that idea since I was also taking on some responsibilities. It appealed to her sense of fairness. Just as I was able to reprimand her whenever she fell short of her objectives, she was able to reprimand me if I fell short.

That approach kept us both honest. Whenever I did not do anything I was supposed to, she was like a hawk and never failed to call me on it. I would always apologize and get it done ASAP. That achieved a couple of things: I showed her how to take responsibility for mistakes made and also validated her perspectives.

She no longer felt "talked down to" and, as such, didn't get defensive whenever I called her on anything.

Hold Her Accountable

Flowing from the previous topic of giving her responsibilities, we must always hold her accountable for having her responsibilities carried out. I keep repeating, you cannot let up. There are no days off for you. If you take the foot off the gas, the car will stop moving.

How to Deal with Sex and Drugs

THIS IS PROBABLY the most sensitive topic to write about. We all like to think our babies are little angels who are innocent to the ways of the world and will guard their carnal treasure until they are married. However, I hope you know that view is extremely misguided and could be downright dangerous.

This is the age of smartphones with unlimited data. You may try to install internet monitoring software on her phone, but she has friends. There was a move called *Demolition Man* with Sylvester Stallone and Wesley Snipes based on a dystopian future where there was an attempt to eliminate crime. Wesley Snipes was a bad guy who was genetically modified to be unable to kill his boss. When he realized that, he just threw the gun to his friend who did not have that modification and ordered him to kill the guy. Hope you get the point. Trying to keep our babies away from sex is like holding our hands up to another incoming wave.

As I learned in lifeguard class, swimming against a current can get you killed. To escape, you have to swim within and across. (If you get nothing else from this book, at least you know what to do in case you get caught in that situation.) Taking that analogy, don't hold your hand up to the incoming wave. She will find out no matter what you do.

Let's try to understand how and why.

Where Will She First Learn about It?

If you were part of a stable relationship, she may have been lucky to learn about sex from you and her mom. If you were a loving couple and loving parents, you and your significant other may have had the talk with her as soon as she was able to understand. You both could have been patient and answered all of her questions and created an atmosphere where she felt comfortable. You could have set a great example with public displays of affection—not R-rated, of course. That is ideal, but who are we kidding? That didn't happen to us. Otherwise, why are you reading this book?

More than likely, she first learned about sex and drugs from her peers. Remember, teenagers think they know everything and we know nothing, so her peers represent the gold standard of education and the gravitas of their tens of months of experience.

In the age of ubiquitous internet, it's difficult to browse the web without tripping over porn. Porn gives an extremely unrealistic view of sex and may be even worse than what she would have heard from her peers.

Or she may come across sex on her own. For example, she may find your porn stash—you need to be more careful—or the internet.

Why Would She Try Them?

She may have a desire to fit in, if all of her friends say they are doing it—I stress the word "say," since teenagers could be like fishermen when it comes to spinning a story. As we know, she has a deep desire to belong, and if that is what it takes, so be it.

There could be peer pressure, which we are all familiar with. If she doesn't have that strong enough sense of self, she could be highly susceptible.

If you are overly strict, she could do it just as an act of defiance, knowing it will piss you off. Of course, she won't tell you. She would just have the satisfaction of knowing she defied you.

Or specifically in the case of drugs, it could be a coping mechanism. I have since learned that some people are genetically predisposed to addiction. This means that not everyone who tries drugs will automatically become addicted. This is why it is now treated as an illness.

She may have low self-esteem and/or may

be seeking affection she believes she is missing. If she feels neglected or not respected, she may seek it elsewhere. This sounds almost like a relationship, doesn't it? Well it absolutely is. And as in any relationship, it needs nurturing.

How to Deal with It

As always, I have absolutely no claims to be a professional. These are just some of my experiences, extrapolated from some common-sense solutions:

- Leave judgment at the door.
- Establish two-way communication.
- Understand the root issue.
- Have realistic expectations.

Leave Judgment at the Door

I can't stress this enough. Remember, she is her own person. She may have come from you, but she is not you. She has her own mind and, as such, her own perspectives. Do not try to compare her to you at her age. The world has changed exponentially since then, and she is exposed to far more than we ever were.

Furthermore, she only has you, and you are just one person who, as much as you try, cannot fulfill her every need.

The second she feels like you are judging her, the window of opportunity for communication will automatically be shut and you will have your face pressed against the glass, looking in. Every word henceforth coming out of your mouth will be treated as a lecture, and she most probably won't pay any attention to a word you are saying.

What could be worse is that you may not even realize it is happing. She may be looking at you and seem to be paying attention, but it's just a vacant stare.

Remember your body language. She is amazingly perceptive, and even though you may say you are not judging her, she can clearly see through you. You have lived with her all her life, and she knows you better than you think.

Establish Two-Way Communication

As we just said, she must not feel like you are judging her. That is one of the most effective two-way communication killers. Remember, she sees herself as a young adult deserving of respect, so you need to listen to what she has to say and really make an effort to see her point of view.

Remember, judging is a communication killer. She needs to feel comfortable enough to speak her truth. I would recommend neutral territory. If I needed to be a disciplinarian, I would have her come to my room. Because that was my domain, it was more intimidating. Find somewhere neutral where she can relax. Remember, she does not feel that she needs to talk to you; therefore, she has something you want and it has to be given willingly or it will have no value.

Don't expect her to spill the beans immediately. You have to earn her trust, and she must feel free to open up. If you already have that kind of relationship, you are ahead of the game. If you don't, you may have to work on that first. If the relationship has generally been one of you dictating, you will have a greater challenge.

Understand the Root Cause of the Issue

The only way you can get to the root cause of the issue is by establishing two-way communication. You cannot force it from her. If you try, she will just lie to you—yes, our babies lie to us from time to time. Self-interest trumps all.

If you were lucky and able to establish true two-way communication and got her to open up, then you can truly listen and get to the root cause of the issue. You can then address that.

Have Realistic Expectations

I say "have realistic expectations" because, as I said before, she has her own mind and, in the end, will do what she feels she needs to do. We are in an advisory role at this point, trying to exercise our influence. If we cultivated good relationships in childhood, that path will be less difficult. However, if that has not been done, it will be an uphill battle.

Don't get me wrong, establishing good relationships since childhood does not automatically fix things. It just makes approaching her easier.

We cannot force her to do what's right. The most we can hope for is that she is willing to give us a window into her world, where we are able to impart some targeted advice.

How to Introduce Her to Your New Relationships

THIS IS NOT the easiest thing in the world. You are the man in her life, and for a while, she has been the only female in yours. Getting her to accept that she has to share you with someone else is not going to be easy. When my daughter realized I was going on a date, she flat-out told me that she thought I was too old and that I had already lived my life. My life should now be dedicated to her. I'm glad she was kind and didn't tell me how she really felt.

I will break down this chapter according to the following topics:

- Going out on dates
- Making the introduction
- Handling when she doesn't like the person
- Handling when your date doesn't like her
- Setting the new normal

Going Out on Dates

We are social creatures and all need companionship. As such, the day will come when we meet someone we want to see beyond a casual basis, be it someone we met on the train, in the office or at a Best Buy on Black Friday (don't judge me). Wait, I forgot, we are in the age of social media, so I will add online.

Even before that happens, I would suggest you take a look inward, and if you have not come to the realization yet, do it now: your life at home with your girl comes first. Anything else is just gravy. If you are not there yet, I would strongly suggest you say it to yourself until it rings true. If you don't, you will be in for some rough roads ahead. Therefore, the first step is to work on you and get your flippin' priorities straight.

Also remember that even though it rings true for you, it must also ring true for her. Therefore, in addition to working on yourself, you must also make sure you are working on the relationship with her so she knows.

Once that is out of the way, you will then have "the talk" with her. She is not an idiot, so don't even try to hide the fact that you are going out on a date. Think about it, could she hide the fact that she likes someone from you? If you do that, it could foster mistrust and set an example that it is ok for her to do the same. Treat her with the same level of honesty you would expect from her. I cannot stress this enough; you must reassure her that she is and always will be number one. It won't be a magic bullet, but it will make the process easier.

If she asks how the date went, you can use it as a good teaching experience. Of course, you won't tell her too much detail, but give her enough to show that you treated your date with respect, paid attention to them, showed up on time, and so on. It will set the level of expectation of what she should expect in someone who wants to date her. By doing that, you can get two for one. Isn't that great?

Making the Introduction

If you are at the stage where you are not looking for anything serious (in the "Tinder" stage), I would just give her high-level details, and only if she asks. Having a stream of dates passing through her life could be destabilizing.

This may be common sense, or then again, maybe not, but I would only think about making the introduction when I see the possibility of something longer term. Only then should you contemplate taking that step. Consider the introduction an interview. As such, you should prep your date. You don't have to prep them about where they see themselves in the next five years; however, since no one knows your girl better than you, it should be easy to prep.

You also want to prep your girl, and at this point, I will refer to what I said in an earlier paragraph about making sure she knows she is number one, remember?

I would suggest meeting in neutral territory, such as a restaurant or park, where conversation could be easy. A movie theater would be a no-no. You wouldn't want to conduct an interview during *The Avengers*, right? Your home would give your girl the advantage in addition to making your date uncomfortable. This is also a no-no.

They should already be familiar with each other since you would have been telling them about each other frequently (hint, hint). Regarding talking to them about each other, remember, their opinion will be clouded by whatever you said before. Therefore, make sure you don't just whine to your date about all of the crap your daughter gives you. You should have been speaking about all of her good qualities as well and how proud you are. Also, make sure your daughter is clear on how you feel about your date and how much you would like them to get along. There's no guarantee it will work, but it will help avert disaster.

I know this divorced couple with two kids. The divorce wasn't exactly amicable; therefore, they did everything they could to undermine each other. The problem occurred when it came to disciplining the kids. Since they each maligned each other and were virtual islands when it came to communicating, the kids were easily able to play one against the other. The more serious complication occurred when it came to discipline. Since neither parent respected the other, the kids didn't respect them in return. Hope you get my point.

Handling When She Doesn't Like the Person

What if after all of your prep and hard work, your daughter gets home and gives you the look? You know the look. It's the look of disapproval your mother gave you when you came home with your fashionable hairstyle. You know the one, Flock of Seagulls, braids, or whatever. You knew this was a possibility, so don't panic. Well don't panic yet. First, get her to talk about it. When she starts talking, really listen, because you want to know the real reason, not the one she tells you to make it easier.

If you realize it's coming from insecurity, you have to double down on reassuring her. Of course, if she tells you that she saw her profile on Tinder saying "down for anything," you may want to reconsider. She may have some valid reasons, such as your date is monopolizing your time, which is to be expected at the beginning of a relationship. However, since you have responsibilities at home, you have to be cognizant of that fact.

You must try to accommodate her as far as reasonable. I stress the word "reasonable." If you realize it's just coming from a selfish place, gently call her out, and in the context of making sure she knows she is number one, tell her that this is a part of your life that she needs to accept. She will always come first, but you deserve to be happy too.

Handling When Your Date Doesn't Like Her

Hopefully you are dating an adult; therefore, you can have a candid conversation. Your date probably won't directly tell you that, but hopefully you will be sensitive enough to pick up on it. I already do not claim to be an expert on little girls, and I know even less about the older ones. Therefore, take this with a huge grain of salt.

If you want the relationship to proceed, you must have the conversation. Don't shy away from it—just rip the Band-Aid off. Better to have the conversation sooner than down the road when you are really committed. If it's something that can be fixed, work on it. If it can't, remember, your girl is number one.

Setting the New Normal

The new normal could range from you dating one special person to you going out on several dates a week. I can't stress enough, make sure everything at home is taken care of and your girl has no doubt she is number one.

Schedule your dates around your life with her as far as reasonable. You may be surprised to know that your dates will respect you more. Nothing is sexier than a man who takes care of home. Also, your girl will gradually come to accept it. If she sees it is making you happy, then she will eventually be happy for you.

How to Deal with the Roller Coaster of Emotional Issues

AS WE ALL know, with the accelerated hormonal changes, she will be experiencing extreme mood swings. Generally, they are just temporary fluctuations, but sometimes they could signal something deeper. As always, I am no professional, but I just take the common-sense approach to the issues I have experienced.

These are the areas that come to mind:

- Depression or anxiety
- Disorders like bulimia and cutting

- Failed relationships
- Disagreements with friends

Depression or Anxiety

Since she is a work in progress and since becoming the self-assured, confident adult like we are (yeah, right) takes time, there will be times when she is unsure of herself and will experience depression and/or anxiety.

The best preventative measure for this is to give her a good sense of self-worth. Note, I am not an advocate of the "participation trophy" methodology where everything is celebrated to the point where she has an exaggerated unrealistic sense of self. Just recognize the things she has done well, tell her how proud you are when she does well, and encourage her to acknowledge her failures and learn from them instead of falling into self-recrimination.

When she gets depressed, you will be tempted to try to cheer her up. Help her get her mind off things. This is not a bad thing, but it's just putting a Band-Aid on the wound without first disinfecting it. The best thing is to get her to talk about it. You cannot force her to do this. It has to happen naturally. Pouring more water on a rose will not make it open any faster.

Sometimes she may not want to talk generally, or she may not want to talk to you specifically. If she doesn't want to talk to you, it could be because she feels uncomfortable sharing something that personal, or she may feel that you may judge her.

If she doesn't want to talk to you specifically, try to determine the reason. Based on the reason, you may have to evaluate how you interact with her and determine if you are to blame. Remember, she is growing up, and if you have not made the transition from dictating to guiding, that could be a reason. Whether or not her reason makes sense to you, just suck it up. It makes sense to her, and at that moment, it's all about her.

Sometimes the problem could be you. Yes I said it! If the problem is you, then you have to work on how you interact with her. Yes, I know, you have to pick up after her and she is showing no sense of responsibility, which is why you still feel like you have to treat her like a child. However, this is like the abusive husband who tells his wife that he really doesn't want to do what he does but she makes him do it by her actions. I am not saying her actions are excusable, but you just have to deal with them the right way. When she was a child, she didn't understand reason; therefore, your approach was what it was. She is beginning to understand reason now; therefore, your approach has to be modified.

Sometimes she just doesn't want to talk, period. We have all been there. If that's the case, just let her be. However, make sure she knows you are there to listen whenever she is ready. Sometimes just a quiet hug can help more than you know.

I remember, once, my daughter was really upset over something. I can't remember what it was specifically, but I remember her walking out of the house and standing outside crying. I went out and hugged her. She just held me, sobbing, and as luck would have it, rain started pouring down at that moment.

I can tell you now that I am not a poet who appreciated the symbolism of the moment. I was standing there, cold and wet, and what did she do? She sat down on the front step. What the heck! So I resisted the urge to tell her to get her crying behind inside. Instead, I sat down next to her and let her cry it out. After about fifteen water-drenched minutes, she felt better to go back inside. I didn't press her or judge her. I just let her cry it out.

When she is anxious about something, the temptation is to encourage her to avoid the situation. However, this is not always the best approach and, in some cases, may make things worse. This is another time to treat the root cause and not just the symptoms.

This is a confusing time, and she is trying to figure out who she is. Therefore, she most probably will not have a strong sense of self. She wants more than anything to be liked, accepted, and validated. Therefore, the foundation begins with you. With you, she must feel all of those things, and from that foundation, she can go forth.

Pay attention to your interactions. You have known her all her life, and with that familiarity comes taking things for granted. Do you dismiss her petty complaints as the ramblings of a child? Do you lose patience with her quickly? Do you still speak to her as if she is eight? Remember, she is transitioning into a woman, and this is a gradual process. Some of the child will still be in there. You should be focusing on the woman you want her to be and not the child you no longer want her to be. Pay attention to the way you treat her.

Sometimes nothing works. Pay attention to whether her depression and anxiety comes and goes or if they are more permanent, which may indicate something deeper. There is no shame in asking for help. There are too many bad things happening to teenage girls—in fact, teenagers in general—that could be prevented if we ask for help in time.

Disorders like Eating, Cutting, Etcetera

When her depression and anxiety metastasizes into something more serious, such as a disorder, this is definitely beyond your level of expertise (or mine). Seek professional help. Do not dismiss it and hope it will pass. You have to be vigilant and take action as soon as those symptoms manifest themselves. The earlier you can identify these issues and seek help, the better.

Failed Relationships

As long as we are breathing, we all will get our hearts broken at some point in our lives, sometimes more than once. It's better to have this happen as early as possible because the later it happens in life, the more devastating—not to mention expensive—it can be. (Think divorce, division of assets, custody of children, etcetera.) If it happens to her while she is at that stage and she is willing to share it with you, it is like striking gold since you will be there to help her deal with it properly and point out the lessons from it. Thomas Edison said that he had not failed but had just found ten thousand ways it won't work—a good perspective to remember.

If you are lucky enough and she shares it with you, do not treat it lightly. How you teach her to handle this is a life lesson that will stay with her always.

Make sure you listen, I mean really listen. The reasons for the breakup may sound trivial to us, but to her, it's the end of the world. Treat it with the respect it deserves. You must validate her during the process. She must know she is being heard. Put yourself in her shoes, and do not judge her.

Sometimes she may want your opinion, and sometimes she may not. Sometimes she may just need to vent. Refrain from passing judgment and telling her what she should have done. Any feedback should be given in the form of advice she is free to accept or discard. In matters of the heart, people have to come to their own realizations.

I remember one time, my daughter brought home this guy I knew was bad news. I would cringe every time I saw him, and I knew she was making the biggest mistake of her life. I saw things going downhill, and she still stayed with him, even though it was really bad for her. I could have stepped in and told her she was forbidden to see him. The only thing that would have accomplished would have been to push her closer to him. She would have continued seeing him and just hidden it from me.

As I mentioned in an earlier chapter, I dated someone in my youth whose dad was the best thing that happened to me. The main reason we got together was because her dad really didn't like me and tried to keep us apart. I kept that lesson with me.

However, in the case of my daughter, I would point out the red flags I saw and the possible consequences. I did not forbid her to see him. I just made my observations and let things happen. My reasoning was to raise her awareness and give her the tools to interpret different aspects of his behavior when they arose.

The longer the relationship persisted, the more annoyed I got. I did not share my annoyance, however. I held my tongue. I made sure she and I were able to maintain a dialogue. Had I flipped out, that avenue to impart any influence would have been shut off to me. It also would have delayed the inevitable of them breaking up because her pride would have been in the picture. I wanted her to feel free to come back whenever she could and not be subjected to the "I told you so" speech.

Eventually, he messed up so badly that she couldn't ignore it. She came back, and because I was not judgmental during the relationship, she felt comfortable telling me all about it. At that time, I was able to help her learn the lessons she needed to learn from the experience.

I then took that opportunity to point out all of his red flags, what they meant, how it affected the relationship, and how to spot them in the future. Yup, I wanted to make sure the memory of that guy was buried deep in the dirt.

Disagreements with Friends

Friendship is just a different type of relationship, and similar principles apply. Make sure you listen, and do not trivialize her issues. Do not judge. Put yourself in her shoes. Make sure she understands the importance of friendship and the impact friends can have on her life. You cannot choose her friends, but you can point out the effect a bad friend can have. Once again, she can accept or reject your observations.

When she has an argument with her friends, sometimes the best thing you can do is not get involved and let them work it out themselves. That's part of the learning process. Validate her, but you don't have to always take her side. Be impartial. If she is wrong, point it out—not in an accusatory kind of way, you are merely pointing out observations.

Make sure she understands that friendship is more important than pride and that there is no shame in admitting when she has made a mistake. On this point, make sure you are living what you are saying. Do you admit when you are wrong? Do you apologize to her when you have made a mistake, or do you think she is just a child and you don't need to? If you are not living it, you can tell her until you run out of breath, but she will never do it.

Someone once told me the phrase "sister before mister." For the sake of being politically correct, we won't mention the male equivalent. Romantic relationships come and go, but friends will always have your back. She should put her friends first just like you put her first, right?

She should also know when keeping a friendship is more than it's worth. I've seen my daughter cut people loose because they made her unhappy. She can be brutal that way. Fortunately, I have never had to teach her that lesson. You may not be so lucky.

As always, the advice you give her will fall on deaf ears if you are not displaying those qualities within yourself. Therefore, take a good look at yourself before you say anything. This could be a good opportunity for introspection, and in helping her, you may actually help yourself.

What to Do When Nothing Works

I WOULD LIKE to say that after you've read and followed the previous chapters, she will make a miraculous transformation and all will be well. Unfortunately, we live in the real world. The arc of her character development will not suddenly bend toward good sense.

You may get frustrated and want to throw up your hands. The main piece of advice I can give is to never give up. This is a transitory part of her life, and only a small fraction of it. We are not defined by the worst thing we have ever done, and she will not be defined by her teenage behavior, which has been brought about by inexperience.

She has the rest of her life ahead of her, and the repercussions of how this transitory period is handled will reverberate for the rest of her life.

Life is the ultimate classroom, and for a significant part of that time, you are her main professor. You cannot for any reason abdicate that responsibility to other teenagers, smartphones, social media, TV, or the internet.

Work on your mission statement, and keep the faith. As adults, we have the advantage of experience. We know there is light at the end of the tunnel. For her, all she sees is what's right before her. There is no tomorrow. Every issue is magnified. You are the one to make her pause, fly up to ten thousand feet, and put things into perspective.

There will be times when she will stray from the path—sometimes farther than you would like. Everything in her life is in transition. However, you have to be that constant that she can always come back to: her true north. As long as she knows that you are there, she will never be truly lost.

You have to get a window into her world and keep it open. Issuing judgments and edicts will only result in her withdrawing from you and seeking advice elsewhere. She has to feel comfortable telling you what's going on in her life, and you must listen without judgment.

If you can do these things, you have a shot.

Lightning Source UK Ltd.
Milton Keynes UK
UKHW010649031121
393296UK00002B/458

9 781977 217189